OPPORTUNITIES DENIED, OPPORTUNITIES DIMINISHED

RACIAL DISCRIMINATION IN HIRING

URBAN INSTITUTE REPORT 91–9

Margery Austin Turner, Michael Fix, and Raymond J. Struyk

with Veronica M. Reed,
Amina H.N. Elmi,
Wendy Zimmermann,
and John G. Edwards

THE URBAN INSTITUTE PRESS
Washington, D.C.

THE URBAN INSTITUTE PRESS

2100 M Street, N.W.
Washington, D.C. 20037

Library of Congress Cataloging in Publication Data

Opportunities Denied, Opportunities Diminished: Racial Discrimination in Hiring/Margery Austin Turner, Michael Fix, and Raymond J. Struyk.

1. Discrimination in employment—United States—Case studies. 2. Race discrimination—United States—Case studies. 3. Afro-American youth—Employment—Illinois—Chicago. 4. Afro-American youth—Employment—Washington (D.C.) I. Fix, Michael. II. Struyk, Raymond J. III. Title. IV. Series.

HD4903.5.U58T87	1991	91-21384
331.13'3'0973—dc20		CIP

(Urban Institute Reports; 91-9, ISSN 0897-7399)

ISBN 0-87766-553-2 (cloth)
ISBN 0-87766-554-0 (paper)

Printed in the United States of America.

Distributed by University Press of America

4720 Boston Way	3 Henrietta Street
Lanham, MD 20706	London WC2E 8LU
	ENGLAND

*U*rban Institute Reports are designed to provide rapid dissemination of research and policy findings. Each report contains timely information and is rigorously reviewed to uphold the highest standards of policy research and analysis.

The Urban Institute is a nonprofit policy research and educational organization established in Washington, D.C., in 1968. Its staff investigates the social and economic problems confronting the nation and government policies and programs designed to alleviate such problems. The Institute disseminates significant findings of its research through the publications program of its Press. The Institute has two goals for work in each of its research areas: to help shape thinking about societal problems and efforts to solve them, and to improve government decisions and performance by providing better information and analytic tools.

Through work that ranges from broad conceptual studies to administrative and technical assistance, Institute researchers contribute to the stock of knowledge available to public officials and private individuals and groups concerned with formulating and implementing more efficient and effective government policy.

Conclusions or opinions expressed in Institute publications are those of the authors and do not necessarily reflect the views of other staff members, officers or trustees of the Institute, advisory groups, or any organizations that provide financial support to the Institute.

Acknowledgments

This report presents the results of The Urban Institute's Employment Discrimination Study (EDS), which was funded by the Rockefeller Foundation. The authors gratefully acknowledge the advice and comments of Genevieve Kenney, Doug Wissoker, and Peter Rossi, all of whom reviewed a draft version of this report. In addition, assistance in audit design and implementation was provided by Harry Cross, Cliff Schupp, and Roderick Boggs, and advice on advanced statistical procedures was provided by John Marcotte and John Yinger.

Our greatest thanks are owed to the 20 young men who served as "testers" for this study, applying for an average of 50 jobs each, and painstakingly recording their treatment at every state in the hiring process. Their commitment to the integrity and objectivity of this research effort was key to the study's success.

CONTENTS

Figure

Abstract

This pilot study seeks to fill the gap in empirical evidence concerning the extent and character of hiring discrimination in the United States. It represents the first attempt to directly measure differential treatment of white and black job seekers applying for entry-level positions. A total of 476 hiring audits were conducted in Washington, D.C. and Chicago during summer 1990. The audit methodology employed was that used for over a decade in housing discrimination studies, and pioneered in the employment context by a 1989 Urban Institute study of discrimination against Hispanic job seekers. Ten pairs of young men—one black, one white—were carefully matched on all characteristics that could affect a hiring decision. They applied for entry-level jobs advertised in the newspaper, and reported their treatment at every stage of the hiring process.

The hiring audit demonstrates that unequal treatment of black job seekers is entrenched and widespread. In one out of five audits, the white applicant was able to advance farther through the hiring process than his black counterpart. In one out of eight audits, the white was offered a job although his equally qualified black partner was not.

In contrast, black auditors advanced farther than their white counterparts only 7 percent of the time, and received job offers while their white partners did not in 5 percent of the audits.

The results indicate that unfavorable treatment of black job seekers is widespread, and that discrimination contributes to black male unemployment and nonparticipation in the labor force. The authors argue that this evidence indicates that pressures to dismantle the machinery of civil rights enforcement are premature.

Executive Summary

Despite the substantial ground black men have gained over the past 25 years relative to white men with regard to wages, income, and access to managerial positions, almost no progress has been made in labor force participation and unemployment rates. The reasons for this have not been supported by systematic evidence, since most research on discrimination in employment has focused on relative wage rates rather than on the hiring process. As results from the current study indicate, discrimination at the hiring stage may well represent the more pressing issue in employment today.

This study is the first to directly measure differential treatment of white and black job seekers applying for entry-level employment. A total of 476 hiring audits were conducted in Washington, D.C. and Chicago during summer 1990. The study employed the "audit" methodology, used for over a decade to test for housing discrimination, and pioneered in the employment context by a 1989 Urban Institute study of discrimination against Hispanic job seekers. Ten pairs of young men—each pair consisting of a black and white—were carefully matched on all characteristics that could affect a hiring decision, and were trained to behave as similarly as possible in an interview setting. They applied for entry-level jobs advertised in the newspaper, and each applicant reported his treatment at every stage of the hiring process.

The hiring audit demonstrates that unequal treatment of black job seekers is entrenched and widespread, contradicting claims that hiring practices today either favor blacks or are effectively color blind. Specifically, in one out of five audits, the white applicant was able to advance farther through the hiring process than his equally qualified black counterpart. In other words, the white was able to submit an application, receive a formal interview, or be offered a job when the black was not. Overall, in one out of eight—or 15 percent—of the audits, the white was offered a job although his equally qualified black partner was not.

In contrast, black auditors advanced farther than their white counterparts only 7 percent of the time, and received job offers while their white partners did not in 5 percent of the audits. In sum, when equally qualified black and white candidates competed for a job, differential treatment, when it occurred, was three times more likely to favor the white applicant than the black.

Overall levels of discrimination differed between the two metropolitan areas studied. Despite the presence of the federal government and its longstanding equal opportunity policies, the incidence of unfavorable treatment was substantially higher in Washington than in Chicago: whites advanced farther than their black counterparts 23 percent of the time in Washington, compared to 17 percent of the time in Chicago.

The study's findings indicate that unfavorable treatment of black job seekers is widespread, and that discrimination contributes to black male unemployment and nonparticipation in the labor force. The results also contradict the view that reverse discrimination is commonplace. Evidence from both this audit and The Urban Institute's 1989 audit of employment discrimination against Hispanic job seekers indicates that pressures to dismantle the machinery of civil rights enforcement are premature. Indeed, the prevalence of disparate treatment in the hiring process means that greater efforts are needed to detect discrimination and to provide victims with access to justice.

The authors conclude that the next logical step is to design and implement a nationwide employment audit for both blacks and Hispanics. Like the national fair housing audit studies sponsored by the U.S. Department of Housing and Urban Development in 1977 and 1989, a full-scale hiring audit would provide statistically reliable estimates of the incidence of discrimination in hiring for the nation as a whole.

Chapter

1

Background and Introduction

There is little evidence, based on direct observation, concerning the extent and character of hiring discrimination in the United States. Specifically, little is known about how often minorities are treated less favorably than equally qualified majority job applicants. Despite this fact, beliefs about employment discrimination's scope and impact are fervently held—as debate over HR 1, the Civil Rights Act of 1991, makes clear. The result is that "much of the debate over the future of civil rights in employment is characterized by high ratios of rhetoric to fact" (Donohue and Siegelman 1991).

This report presents the findings of the Employment Discrimination Study, a pilot study measuring the extent of unfavorable treatment experienced by young black males applying for entry-level jobs in two metropolitan areas. Data were obtained from "hiring audits" conducted in Chicago and Washington, D.C., in the summer of 1990. Briefly, the findings indicate that, in the two metropolitan areas studied, young black job seekers were unable to advance as far in the hiring process as their white counterparts 20 percent of the time; black testers advanced farther than their white counterparts 7 percent of the time. In addition, blacks were denied a job that was offered to an equally qualified white tester 15 percent of the time; white testers were denied a job when their black counterparts received an offer in 5 percent of the audits.

HR 1, the Civil Rights Act of 1991, is the successor to legislation passed by the U.S. Congress in 1990 but vetoed by President George Bush. The 1990 and 1991 bills represent a congressionally led effort to restore and extend protections for employees and job applicants that were limited by a series of decisions handed down by the U.S. Supreme Court in its 1988 and 1989 terms. Those Court decisions are consistent with much of the administrative (versus congressional) policymaking that has taken place in the civil rights field over the past decade. That is, both judges and administration policymakers have taken as their point of departure the belief that American society has made great progress in combatting discrimination and that the nation is well on the way to becoming a color-blind society. These assumptions are supported by some scholars who claim that most overt discrimination has been eliminated (e.g., Strauss 1990) and by others who argue that the residual discrimination is not worthy of "elimination by state coercion" (e.g., Epstein 1990).

In fact, however, there is no empirical evidence that discrimination has been eliminated, and the belief that it has been substantially eradicated is not universally endorsed, even by moderate and conservative lawmakers. For example, Supreme Court Justice Harry Blackmun, dissenting in *Wards Cove Packing Co. v. Atonio* (1989)—perhaps the most far-reaching Court opinion on employment rights to emerge from the 1988 term[1]—stated: "[O]ne wonders whether the majority still believes that race discrimination—or, more accurately, race discrimination against nonwhites—is a problem in our society, or even remembers that it ever was."

The concerns of those who suspect that discrimination persists have been reinforced by public opinion data developed by the National Opinion Research Center (NORC) at the University of Chicago. Although opinion research has consistently revealed a steady decline in prejudice among Americans,[2] the report released by the NORC in January 1991 found that *a majority* of whites still believe that both blacks and Hispanics are not only more inclined than whites to prefer welfare, but are also lazier, more prone to violence, less intelligent, and less patriotic. Although these responses do not represent evidence of discriminatory attitudes or behavior by employers, they do "easily disabuse the belief that Americans are approaching a color and creed blind society..." (Smith 1990). Further, these racial and ethnic images are "significant predictors of support for racial integration programs ... and desired social distance."

Recent data on worker perceptions also raise concerns about the possible persistence of discrimination in employment. A 1990 random survey of 803 adults commissioned by the *National Law Journal* (Swoboda 1990) revealed the perception of pervasive discrimination. Fifty-one percent of those interviewed—48 percent of whites and 64 percent of blacks—said that all or most "employers practice some form of discrimination in their hiring and promotion practices, regardless of their official policies." In addition, 5 percent of white respondents and 25 percent of black respondents believed they had been discriminated against on the basis of race or ethnicity; 23 percent of whites and 36 percent of blacks believed they had been discriminated against for this or other reasons.[3]

Finally, a recent survey of employers in Chicago focused explicitly on employer perceptions of blacks and their attractiveness as job candidates (Kirschenman and Neckerman 1991). This study found that employers consistently relate race to inferior education, lack of job skills, and unreliable job performance. The authors concluded that "Chicago's employers did not hesitate to generalize about race or ethnic differences in the quality of the labor force. Most associated negative images with inner-city workers, and particularly with black men."

Employment Discrimination and Joblessness among Black Males and Youth

Evidence of the economic gains of black males, like evidence of attitudinal change, reveals uneven progress. The economic status of black men relative to white men has improved along a number of dimensions in the past 20 years: the wage gap has narrowed, the share of black men working as managers and professionals has increased, and the share of black men whose income exceeds the white median tripled between 1939 and 1979 (Heckman and Verkerke 1990). In the 1980s, some further narrowing of the earnings gap between blacks and whites occurred among those working, but this was accompanied by a sharp reduction in black male labor force participation rates, especially for those with low levels of education. Thus, the extent of blacks' overall progress in recent years is ambiguous (Jaynes 1990).

These negative employment trends are even more pronounced among black male youths, where the relative rate of joblessness (42 percent versus 19 percent for white male youths) is strikingly high.[4] These high rates of joblessness mean that too many young black men will never gain a foothold in the "formal economy"—a fact that imposes severe costs on them and the society as a whole.

Rees (1986) advanced three hypotheses to explain high rates of joblessness among young black males—hypotheses that may also explain differing levels of labor force participation for the black male population as a whole. They include:

- Entry-level jobs are moving away from the inner city, leaving blacks with reduced access to employment opportunities in comparison with their white counterparts;

- Employers discriminate against black youth in the hiring process, so that blacks are rejected from jobs that are available; and

- Young black men are poorly qualified for employment, owing either to the inferior quality of central city schools or because the social milieu of these youths gives low priority to the attributes that lead to school or job performance.

All three of these possible explanations have proven difficult or impossible to test empirically with much rigor. Recent analyses of job suburbanization or deconcentration have generated the most robust findings, indicating that this "spatial mismatch" is having an increasingly large impact on black employment (Holzer 1989). Using data from the Philadelphia metropolitan area, Ihlanfeldt and Sioquist (1990) estimated that between 30 percent and 50 percent of the employment gap between black and white youth can be explained by job accessibility. Supporting data are also presented for Chicago and Los Angeles.[5]

Assuming that these estimates assign the correct order of magnitude to decentralization, the majority of the difference between joblessness or employment rates of blacks and whites still remains unexplained. Obviously, differences in schooling and training are important factors. So also are differing levels of participation in the underground or drug economy (Reuter et al. 1990), the devastating employment consequences of serving time in prison (Freeman 1990), the availability of entry-level jobs that require comparatively low skills and education (Bendick and Egan 1988), and the number, policies and effectiveness of job-training programs (Gregory 1988). Nevertheless, the question remains: to what degree does hiring discrimination explain residual differences?

Although there is an extensive literature on black and white wage differentials and the discriminatory practices they may reflect, there has been little empirical investigation of discrimination in hiring, as Donohue and Siegelman (1991) recently noted. As the evidence cited here indicates, more progress has been made in reducing wage differentials between white and black workers than in reducing the gap in labor force participation. As a result, discrimination at the hiring stage may well represent the more pressing issue in employment today.

Analyses of the extent of hiring discrimination may not only explain differing labor force participation rates; they should also help frame remedies to this problem. For example, if it is the case that firms move away from the central city to escape minority workers, then racial and other minorities can expect to be discriminated against if they apply for positions in the suburbs. This scenario, in turn, suggests that attitudinal change and enforcement of antidiscrimination laws should precede, or at any rate accompany, efforts to increase minorities' access to suburban employment. If, on the other hand, minorities are no more likely to encounter discrimination in the suburbs than in the central city, then policymakers can focus on strategies for increasing access to the suburban workplace, while pursuing metropolitan-wide enforcement of employment discrimination protections.

Hiring Audit Methodology

This study employs the "hiring audit" methodology pioneered by Cross et al. (1990) in a parallel study of discrimination against Hispanic job seekers in Chicago and San

Diego. The techniques for conducting hiring audits build directly on the substantial experience developed in the past 15 years in conducting systematic audit studies of discrimination in housing (Turner, Struyk, and Yinger 1990; Wienk et al. 1979).[6]

In a hiring audit, a minority group tester and majority group tester are carefully matched on all attributes that could affect the hiring decision. Specifically, they are paired in terms of age, physical size, education, experience, and other "human capital" characteristics, as well as such intangibles as openness, apparent energy level, and articulateness. While many of these attributes can be assigned for the purposes of the audit (years of school completed and prior work experience, for example), matching others requires very careful assessment and pairing of individual candidates. Once auditors have been matched, an opening for an entry-level job is identified in the local newspaper and each auditor separately attempts to inquire about the position, complete an application, obtain an interview, and be offered the job. The incidence of differential treatment is determined by comparing the experiences and outcomes for the two auditors.

In this study, a total of 476 audits were conducted by 10 pairs of testers. Audits were conducted in Washington, D.C. and Chicago in summer 1990. Although we followed many of the sampling and field procedures used by Cross and his colleagues (1990), we developed more comprehensive measures of differential treatment and employed a different statistical technique for reporting the extent of unfavorable treatment experienced by blacks.[7] Subordinate goals of our study were experimental: to further advance the "technology" of testing in the employment context and to improve tools for analyzing and interpreting the results.

Organization of the Report

Chapter 2 of this report describes key aspects of the study's methodology, including the selection and pairing of auditors, the sampling strategy, and the number and types of jobs audited in each market. Chapter 3 outlines the hiring process and the points at which unfavorable treatment can occur and the forms it may take. Chapter 4 presents our findings and compares them to the results of the Hispanic-Anglo hiring audit conducted in 1989. Finally, the report concludes with a summary of findings and their implications for policy.

Notes, chapter 1

1. *Wards Cove Packing Co. v. Atonio,* 109 S. Ct. 2115 (1989), quoting 2133-36. Among other things, the decision makes it more difficult for plaintiffs in disparate impact cases to establish a prima facie case, reduces the burden on employers once that case has been established, and reduces employers' burden in justifying challenged business practices. See, generally, Belton (1990).

2. For example, Schuman, Steeh, and Bobo (1985) concluded that discriminatory beliefs (e.g., "blacks are inferior to whites") have been steadily declining in the population at large over the past 40 years.

3. Data from Swoboda (1990) and unpublished tabulations of the survey results provided to The Urban Institute.

4. Data presented in Rees (1986), April 1985. Joblessness includes those out-of-school young men who do not have jobs. It differs from unemployment in that it includes the jobless who are not looking for work as well as those who are searching for a position.

5. Ihlanfeldt and Sioquist (1990) have also investigated the effects of decentralization on the earnings of central-city blacks. For a general review of this literature, see Jencks and Mayer (1990).

6. Like its predecessor Hispanic-Anglo hiring audit study, this work is a pilot project to develop the first reliable information on hiring discrimination against black youths and to continue development of a methodology for documenting the incidence and forms of hiring discrimination. There have also been parallel studies conducted in Canada and the United Kingdom, which appear to follow a broadly similar methodology, although actors were used as testers. For a description of the findings, see Reitz (1988).

7. This statistical technique was developed as part of the national Housing Discrimination Study audit project, whose field work was done in 1989. For a description of the basic technique, see Turner et al. (1991).

Chapter

2

Hiring Audit Methodology

This chapter summarizes the basic methodology of the Employment Discrimination Study. Specifically, we discuss the choice of metropolitan areas in which to conduct the study; the way in which job vacancies were sampled; the number of valid audits completed and their distribution in each city among occupations and types of business; and procedures for recruiting, matching, and training auditors at the two sites.

Selecting Metropolitan Areas

Given the experimental character of the project and the resources available, it was clear that statistically significant numbers of audits could be carried out to measure discrimination in two metropolitan areas. This means that our results are not representative of all urban areas or the nation as a whole. Three criteria guided the selection of the two sites:

1. The metropolitan areas had to be major conurbations, each important in its own right so as to make the results of general interest.

2. Each area had to have been included in the 1989 national Housing Discrimination Study, conducted for the U.S. Department of Housing and Urban Development (HUD) by The Urban Institute (Turner et al. 1990). Twenty-five areas were included in the HUD project, all with substantial minority populations.[1] The Employment Discrimination Study would thus contribute to a growing body of information on discrimination in selected metropolitan areas.

3. The two sites had to differ in terms of industrial structure, labor market tightness, demographic composition, and other factors.

Based on these criteria, the Washington, D.C., and Chicago metropolitan areas were selected. Washington, D.C., is the home of the Committee on Strategies to Reduce Chronic Poverty at the Greater Washington Research Center, one of six community planning and action projects funded by the Rockefeller Foundation to examine the conditions of, and seek remedies to, persistent poverty. Extensive analysis has recently been undertaken of the city's poverty population and of the local economy (Carr et al. 1988), raising questions among local leaders about the role of racial discrimination in explaining comparatively low rates of labor force participation among young black males. In part, the present study is an attempt to respond to those questions. Chicago was one of the two sites for The Urban Institute's Hispanic-Anglo hiring study (Cross et al. 1990), enabling us to make approximate comparisons between the level of discrimination against blacks and Hispanics. Both Chicago and Washington are major metropolitan areas, and both were included in the HUD housing audit study (Turner et al. 1990). They also differ sharply from each other in several important respects.

First, Chicago's employment is more heavily concentrated in production jobs and in the sales and service sectors compared to Washington's (see table 2.1). Forty-six percent of Washington's employment is among executives, professional specialty, and technician positions, compared with 30 percent for Chicago. Second, the Washington labor market was, until the summer of 1990, tight and growing, whereas Chicago's has been comparatively loose and stagnant. Over the 1986-88 period, employment in Washington expanded by 6.3 percent compared to 1.6 percent in Chicago. Over the same period, the unemployment rates in the two areas averaged 2.9 and 6.9 percent, respectively.[2] These differences are important because, as Freeman (1990) has demonstrated, black youth unemployment rates are sensitive to overall labor market conditions.

A third difference between Chicago and Washington pertains to the proportion of blacks in the population. In 1980 blacks constituted roughly comparable proportions of the two metropolitan areas' population (20 percent in Chicago, 28 percent in Washington). However, blacks constituted 70 percent of District of Columbia inhabitants compared with 40 percent of those living within the City of Chicago. A fourth difference is that residential racial segregation in the Chicago metropolitan area is greater than that in Washington. For example, on a measure of the extent to which blacks are isolated spatially from whites, Chicago scored 0.828 whereas Washington scored 0.672. (The average score for all metropolitan areas is 0.488.)[3] In fact, Massey and Denton (1989) included Chicago among 10 "hypersegregated" metropolitan areas in the U.S.

One of our initial hypotheses was that residents of the two areas might differ in attitudes toward hiring minorities. In Washington the massive presence of the federal government, which has actively promoted affirmative hiring and other

TABLE 2.1   Percentage Distribution of Employed Male Civilians in the Chicago and Washington, D.C., Metropolitan Areas by Occupation, 1988

	Chicago	Washington, D.C.
Executive, administrative, and managerial	15.1	19.3
Professional specialty	12.7	20.9
Technicians	2.3	5.9
Sales	13.2	9.0
Administrative support, including sales	8.1	8.5
Service occupations	11.8	8.9
Precision production, craft and repair	15.8	14.7
Machine operators, assemblers, and inspectors	7.0	1.7
Transportation and materials moving	6.2	4.7
Handlers, equipment cleans, etc.	7.0	4.1
Total	100.0	100.0

Sources: U.S. Bureau of Statistics (1988, 1989b).

equal opportunity programs for years, might have set a tone for the entire community.[4] Another hypothesis was that employment by black-owned firms would differ between the two areas. However, in 1987, employees of black-owned firms constituted only 1.5 percent of all workers in the Washington area and 0.3 percent in the Chicago area; presumably, therefore, the presence of these firms is not a factor.[5]

The diversity of the two metropolitan areas is a strength of the study. A finding that black youths are substantially discriminated against in both labor markets would *suggest* a pervasive pattern of discrimination in America's urban labor markets and argue for a strong program of auditing and enforcement of equal opportunity laws.

Sampling Job Vacancies

To ensure statistically significant results for both Washington, D.C, and Chicago, we estimated we would need to complete between 200 and 250 audits in each site. Samples of this size are adequate to detect differences of 15 percentage points between white-favored and black-favored outcomes.[6] The sampling process consisted of two separate steps. First, the sample frame was defined. Second, specific job vacancies were drawn from this frame for auditing.

The Sampling Frame

The principal requirement for drawing a random sample is that the universe must be defined so that each job vacancy in the selected occupations has an equal chance of being drawn.[7] In the United States jobs are obtained through: (1) personal contacts; (2) direct application (i.e., a job seeker visits a business in search of work, but is not directed there by an ad or referral); and (3) intermediaries such as newspaper ads and employment services (Holzer 1987b).

In the Hispanic-Anglo audit study, Cross and his colleagues (1990) explored the possibility of developing a sampling frame for the first two job sources and ultimately concluded that this was not feasible. Therefore, they turned to newspaper help-wanted ads. They listed the principal advantages of using newspapers in a short-term hiring audit as:

- Newspaper ads are one of the main sources of employment information used by young adults. Surveys show that 30 percent to 60 percent of young adults use newspaper classified ads as a job-search method (Holzer 1988; U.S. Bureau of Labor Statistics 1989c).[8]

- Newspaper ads, particularly for sales, service, clerical, and blue collar jobs, are roughly representative of the distribution of all job vacancies in broad occupational categories (Abraham 1987).

- As a single source, newspaper classified ads provide centralized access to a large number of jobs (thousands of ads appear every weekend in big-city newspapers). These ads are relatively simple to sample.

- Newspaper ads serve as a productive, low-cost approach for a hiring audit because each ad represents an employer who is presumably ready to make a job hiring decision, in contrast to direct application where employers often let applications languish without any progress or resolution.

- Both minority and majority job seekers can use newspaper ads (i.e., information about the availability of these jobs is open to everyone).

- It is believed that employers who advertise in the newspaper tend to discriminate less than those who hire through personal contact and direct application. Thus, a newspaper classified ad sampling frame provides a conservative, lower-bound estimate of disparate treatment.

We followed Cross et al. (1990) and used the classified ads in each area's major newspaper exclusively as the sampling frame. Not all advertised jobs or advertising employers were included, however. We chose to sample low-skill, entry-level jobs requiring limited experience, because these jobs are typically filled by high school graduates in the 18-24 age range. They include occupations in hotel, restaurant and other services, retail sales, office work, management (mainly trainee positions), technical areas, and general labor, including manufacturing. These low-skill, entry-level occupations represent precisely the types of jobs where the bulk of young adults begin their working careers. The damage done by discrimination at this entry point is compounded by reducing future upward mobility and can discourage young men from even seeking regular employment.

Not all entry-level jobs are appropriate for an audit study. Numerous jobs were judged ineligible by us because they required such credentials as a specialized driver's license or equipment such as a tool chest. Other jobs eliminated were part-time, temporary, and government positions.[9] Also excluded were jobs filled through intermediaries such as an employment service.

Drawing the Sample

Random samples of advertisements for job vacancies were drawn weekly from Sunday issues of the *Washington Post* and the *Chicago Tribune* during a five-week period in early summer 1990. The ads drawn in the sampling procedure each Sunday by the site supervisor were audited the following week. About 60 percent of the ads contained announcements for more than one job opening for the same type of position. In drawing the sample, each advertised position was given an equal chance of being selected, but multiple openings for the same position (e.g., three waiters at one restaurant) were treated as a single position.

Sample Size and Composition

Altogether, 218 valid audits were completed in Chicago and 258 in Washington (table 2.2). These successful audits resulted from 490 and 486 total audits initiated in the two sites, respectively. The initiated audits include, both those drawn in the first sampling on Sunday and replacements to the first sample. About half of the audits initiated resulted in a valid audit. The remaining audits that were initiated proved to be either "ineligible" for inclusion in the sample or "invalid" because (1) the jobs had already been filled, (2) one or both auditors was screened out on the telephone, or (3) the auditors could not make contact with the employer after repeated tries.

TABLE 2.2   Disposition of Sampled Job Vacancies

	Chicago	Washington, D.C.
Initial sample[a]	414	375
Replacements[b]	76	111
Ineligibles and invalids[c]	272	228
Valid audits	218	258

a. Number of ads drawn by initial sampling of the Sunday newspaper.
b. Job vacancies sampled as replacements for initial sample vacancies found to be ineligible. The initial sample plus replacements equals the total number of audits initiated, 490 in Chicago and 486 in Washington.
c. Includes jobs already filled and cases in which both auditors were screened out on the telephone or in which neither auditor could make contact with the employer after repeated tries. Includes ineligible ads from both the initial and replacement samples.

Valid audits include all those in which both auditors appeared in person to submit an application and in which at least one auditor was able to at least submit an employment application. The distribution of valid audits by disposition is shown in table 2.3; almost 90 percent of the audits ran the full course to a possible job offer or denial of a job by the employer. The balance were either terminated somewhere in the process or "truncated" because an employer audited in the final two weeks had not made a job-offer decision by the close of field operations. Terminations occurred when employers required applicants to take tests or attend training sessions or when auditors encountered someone they knew at the job site or reported that employers seemed suspicious of their identities or applications.

TABLE 2.3   Types and Number of Valid Audits

	Chicago	Washington, D.C.	Number	Percent
Completed	191	227	418	88
Valid audits; neither terminated nor truncated				
Terminated	9	10	19	4
Valid audits terminated because of expected events				
Truncated	18	21	39	8
Valid audits started in last two weeks of study in which employer did not make a job offer decision for at least one tester				
Totals	218	258	476	100

As shown in table 2.4, job vacancies audited in both sites were heavily concentrated in the service and retail trade sectors. Interestingly, the difference in the overall industrial composition of the two cities was not reflected in the distribution of entry-level job vacancies advertised. Among the more commonly audited positions in both sites were office support, restaurant help, and retail sales. Comparatively few production jobs were advertised.

TABLE 2.4 Distribution of Audited Positions by Sector and Occupation (percentage of valid audits)

	Chicago	Washington, D.C.
Sector		
Construction	0.9	2.7
Manufacturing	2.8	3.1
Retail trade	31.7	29.8
Service	64.7	65.5
Transportation	0.0	1.6
Occupation		
Services:		
Hotel	11.0	3.9
Other	15.1	3.5
Restaurant	21.6	19.8
Total	47.7	27.2
Sales	26.6	20.2
Office	14.2	26.4
General labor	6.9	18.6
Technical	1.8	0.4
Management	2.8	7.4

Auditor Selection and Training

The hiring audits were conducted by 10 pairs of full-time, paid auditors, 5 pairs in each of the two audit sites.[10] Careful recruitment, matching, and training of auditors was integral to the success of the study. The auditors, one black and one white, were carefully matched to control for all "job-relevant" characteristics. Specifically, these were experience, education, age, and physical strength and size. Audit partners were made identical in a defined set of job qualifications and trained so that other attributes—demeanor, openness, articulateness, and energy level—were as similar as possible. Race was the only important difference between the two members of each audit team.

Male college students between the ages of 19 and 24 were recruited from major universities in the Chicago and Washington, D.C., metropolitan areas. Job announcements seeking research assistants, and accompanied by letters explaining that the sex and age stipulations were bona fide occupational requirements, were mailed to university employment and placement offices, social science departments, minority affairs offices, and select professors. Respondents were screened over the telephone, and all who met the job requirements were invited to apply and received an initial interview. Twenty-three applicants in Washington and thirty-one applicants in Chicago were initially interviewed for the 10 auditor positions in each site. After initial interviews, all qualified applicants were independently interviewed by two additional individuals, consensus was reached about whom to hire, and preliminary audit teams were formed.

Conventional appearance was the major selection criterion—average height, average weight, conventional dialect, and conventional dress and hair. This made audit partners potentially interchangeable, except where we were able to find similarly unique partners. Most auditors were between the ages of 19 and 21 and between 5'8" and 5'10" tall. However, there was a team comprising a 6'4", bearded, twenty-three-year-old white partner and a 6'2", bearded, twenty-four-year-old black partner in Washington. And, in Chicago, there was a team of 24-year-old graduate students who had both studied abroad.

All auditors participated in a five day training session, the overriding goal of which was to make paired auditors as similar as possible. On the first day of training, auditors were videotaped during a mock interview and pairs were finalized by consensus of senior project staff based on similarities in appearance, mannerisms, personality, and interview style.[11] The first day of training also included an introduction to employment discrimination, equal employment opportunity, and a review of project design and methodology. The second day was spent creating the auditors' biographies. The biographies—a record of the auditors' fictitious personas—detailed their personal, school and past employment histories. Most of the auditors posed as recent high school graduates, with limited work experience including summer and after-school jobs as waiters or busboys, parking lot attendants, and file clerks. Some of the older pairs posed as having a maximum of two years' work experience since high school graduation and some community-college course work.

The auditors were required to memorize all information on their biographies. Two days were spent on instructions for conducting an audit, learning a standardized method for filling out job applications, filling out the survey instrument, and completing simulated audits. These simulated audits were critical because they allowed the auditors to experience every stage of the hiring process and to learn to properly complete applications and survey instruments. In these mock audits, the auditors were also able to observe and critique their partners in different interview situations, trainers were able to point out and help minimize differences in the way partners come across to employers, and auditors learned to match their responses in a wide range of circumstances. On the final day of training, the audit pairs went on practice audits, giving them one real audit experience before actual auditing began.

Notes, chapter 2

1. All areas in the Housing Discrimination Study had central cities of over 100,000 population in 1980, and in those in which black-white audits were conducted, blacks constituted at least 12 percent of the 1980 population (the national average percentage of blacks in metropolitan areas).

2. Data from U.S. Bureau of Labor Statistics (1987, 1988, 1989b).

3. Figures from Massey and Denton (1989).

4. Government positions themselves are not included among those audited, however, because the federal hiring process was expected to differ so significantly from that of private employers.

5. Chicago data are for the primary metropolitan statistical area (PMSA) (Cook, DuPage, and McHenry counties), and those for Washington, D.C., are for the standard metropolitan statistical area (SMSA). Data on black employees of black-owned firms are from the U.S. Bureau of the Census (1990), and those on total employment are from the U.S. Bureau of Labor Statistics (1989a).

6. Although this report does not focus on the "net" estimates of discrimination (percentage of white-favored minus percentage of black-favored outcomes), it is nevertheless essential to plan for sample sizes large enough to ensure detectable differences between the share of white-favored and black-favored outcomes.

7. This section draws heavily on Cross et al. (1990: 13-17).

8. For data on sources of information found by all workers in finding jobs, see Corcoran, Datcher, and Duncan (1980).

9. Government jobs obviously account for an important share of the Washington, D.C., job market. Nevertheless, these jobs were excluded because the government hiring process was expected to differ so significantly from that of private employers.

10. All the audit pairs were assigned the same number of advertisements from each week's sample. Their success in completing audits varied somewhat by site and by pair, but, on average, each pair in

Chicago completed 44 audits over a six week period, and each pair in Washington, D.C., completed 52 audits over the same period.

11. Two of the preliminary pairings in Washington, D.C., were changed based on this process.

Chapter

3

The Hiring Process and Forms of Differential Treatment

There are several distinct steps in the hiring process for entry-level positions, and unfavorable treatment can occur at each stage. Unfavorable treatment may be so severe as to make it impossible for an applicant to proceed to the next stage; in these cases, the applicant's employment opportunity is denied. In other cases unfavorable treatment may be less severe but still result in diminished opportunity for the applicant. This chapter outlines the hiring process and our measurement of the ways in which unfavorable treatment may occur within it.

Stages in the Hiring Process

Figure 3.1 summarizes the basic stages in the hiring process for an entry-level position advertised in the newspaper, and indicates the kinds of unfavorable treatment that may occur

FIGURE 3.1 Differential Outcomes and Differential Treatment in the Hiring Process

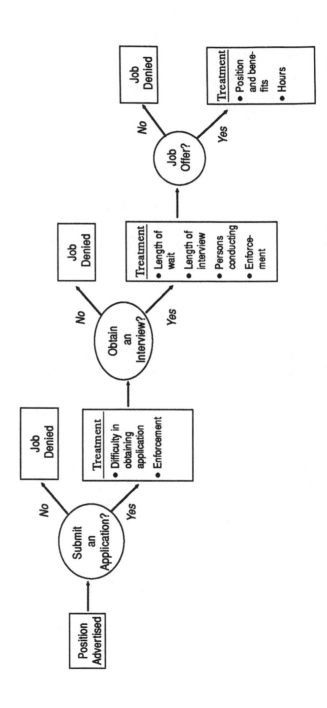

at each stage. The three stages in the hiring process are: submission of an employment application, obtaining an interview with someone in authority at the company, and receiving a job offer. At each stage, an applicant can be severely disadvantaged (compared to his equally qualified audit partner) if he is eliminated from competition for the job: he may be denied the opportunity to complete an application, he may not be granted an interview, or he may be denied a job offer.

The third stage—receiving a job offer—is unique, since it is possible that the employer may only have one position to fill.[1] Audit procedures were designed to minimize the possibility that an employer would offer a job to one member of an audit pair and then consider the job filled, so that the other partner had no chance of receiving an offer. Specifically, auditors were instructed to turn down job offers as soon as possible after they were received, thereby creating the opportunity for their partner to be offered the position. In 41 percent of the audits in which a job offer was made, both team members received an offer. This strongly suggests that "interdependence of outcomes" was not a significant problem.[2]

Denying or Diminishing Opportunities

In the Hispanic-Anglo audit study, Cross et al. (1990) focused exclusively on opportunity denial, tabulating differences in treatment at each of the three stages in the hiring process. In addition, they developed an overall index that reflected cumulative differences in treatment between Anglo and Hispanic auditors as they proceeded through the hiring process. The present study goes beyond this approach by asking if differential treatment, which diminished the applicant's opportunity to obtain the position, occurred at any stage even though it was not severe enough to prevent the job applicant from proceeding to the next stage or receiving a job offer.

Differential treatment that diminishes a job seeker's prospects can be important even though it does not necessarily deny him the opportunity to compete for a job. It is clearly discouraging to an applicant if he consistently encounters adverse treatment in the course of a job search. Examples of such treatment include being asked many questions or being pressed about job qualifications even before receiving an application form, being kept waiting for a long period before a scheduled interview, and being given a brief or perfunctory interview in which little information about the job is presented and the applicant's questions are not treated seriously. At the extreme, young men experiencing this kind of treatment may stop applying for jobs; but short of this, they may learn to sense (or think they sense) that they are being subtly discouraged in the initial contact with a company, possibly even over the telephone, and respond to those signals by not pursuing a position. The result, obviously, is a substantially diminished likelihood of obtaining a job.

Types of differential treatment that diminish opportunity in this way are listed in figure 3.1 for each stage in the process. Of particular importance is differential treatment at the job-offer stage. Even though a minority applicant receives a job-offer, it may be for a lower quality position than that advertised or offered to his audit partner, the pay may be lower, no fringe benefits may be provided, and the working hours and other conditions may be less favorable than for the position advertised or for the job offered to the partner auditor.

The analysis of outcomes presented in the next chapter includes examination of unfavorable treatment at both levels of severity. We have adopted a two-step rule to define differential treatment occurring at each stage in the hiring process. First, if one auditor does not proceed through the step but his partner does, unequal treatment—opportunity denial—is said to have occurred; second, when both partners proceed through the stage, differential treatment is said to have occurred if one auditor is treated unfavorably on more items measuring "diminished opportunity" than his audit partner.

Measuring Unfavorable Treatment

Unfavorable treatment of minority auditors can occur for both systematic and random reasons. Suppose an employer conducted an interview with the white auditor but not with his black partner, so that the audit has been classified as "majority-favored" for this outcome variable. This unfavorable treatment of the black might have occurred for systematic reasons: perhaps the employer is prejudiced and prefers not to hire minorities, or perhaps the work force is predominantly white and the employer fears that hiring a black will create tension, or perhaps the business operates in a predominantly white community and the employer feels that he may lose customers by hiring minority workers. Regardless of the motivation, unfavorable treatment for systematic reasons constitutes discrimination against minority applicants.

However, unfavorable treatment may also result from random factors. For example, the employer might have hired an outstanding applicant between the initial visit by the majority auditor and that of the minority auditor, and therefore saw no point in conducting a formal interview with the minority applicant. Or perhaps the employer felt ill or tired at the time of the minority auditor's visit. Any number of random events might result in unfavorable treatment of a minority applicant that is not systematic, and technically should not be interpreted as discrimination. If unfavorable treatment is the result of random events, then, on another day, the same team would receive equal treatment, and minority applicants seeking jobs from the audited employer would generally be treated fairly. Thus, it would be a mistake to interpret all "majority-favored" outcomes as discrimination, since some of these outcomes reflect truly random events.

Another complicating issue is that, in some audits, the minority auditor rather than the majority auditor receives preferential treatment. Again, both systematic and random events may contribute to these "minority-favored" audits. Suppose, for example, that an employer offered a job to the minority auditor but not to the majority partner. This difference could be the result of random factors. But it might also result from two distinct types of discrimination. Specifically, some cases of "minority-favored" treatment may actually reflect a different form of discrimination. For example, the job offered to a minority auditor might be in a predominantly minority work force or in a category of jobs that the employer views as "reserved" for minorities. Alternatively, a "minority-favored" outcome might reflect preferential treatment of minority customers for systematic reasons. An employer might prefer to hire minorities or to provide the best possible opportunity whenever minorities apply. Thus, cases with "minority-favored" outcomes are particularly difficult to interpret, because they may reflect random events, hidden discrimination of some other kind, or systematically preferential treatment of minority applicants.

It is important to interpret the relationship between white-favored and black-favored outcomes carefully. In the past, it has been a practice to subtract the share of minority-favored audits from the share of majority-favored audits. Our approach, however, is that white-favored and black-favored outcomes both occur, and that each has independent significance. Therefore, the basic measures of differential treatment presented in this report represent the incidence of white-favored outcomes—the share of audits in which black applicants were treated less favorably than equally qualified white job seekers—and the incidence of black-favored outcomes—the share of audits in which blacks received more favorable treatment than their equally qualified white partners.[3]

The decision to focus on this "gross" measure of the incidence of unfavorable treatment is reinforced by findings from a recent large, national audit study of housing discrimination. Advanced statistical procedures employed in that study indicate that the incidence of unfavorable treatment experienced by minorities can be viewed as a realistic approximation of the incidence of systematic discrimination. Specifically, in the national Housing Discrimination Study, sponsored by the U.S. Department of Housing and Urban Development (see Yinger 1991), data from 3,800 audits were analyzed to separate systematic and random components of unfavorable treatment. This analysis produced estimates of discrimination that were consistently close to the levels of unfavorable treatment.[4]

Notes, chapter 3

1. Note that if neither auditor was offered a job (because another candidate is selected) we recorded it as "no difference" in treatment.

2. The same conclusion was reached with respect to the Hispanic-Anglo audits, where auditors obtained offers in half of the audits, and in 41 percent of these cases both auditors received offers. For more details, see Cross et al. (1990: 48-50).

3. Appendix A describes the methodology used to test the statistical significance of these results, taking into account the fact that outcomes are observed for "clusters" of black and white job applicants.

4. We elected to draw upon these results for guidance in interpreting our findings rather than conduct similar analyses with our data set because of the vastly larger sample size in the housing study and because Yinger was able to estimate a fully-specified model while we would not have been able to do so with the data available to us.

4

Unfavorable Treatment of Black Job Seekers

Young black men applying for entry-level jobs face a substantial chance of being treated less favorably than comparable white applicants. In 20 percent of the audits conducted in Washington, D.C., and Chicago, the white applicant advanced farther in the hiring process than his black counterpart, and in 15 percent the white applicant was offered a job whereas his equally qualified black partner was not. Blacks were favored over comparable white applicants in a much smaller share of cases; in 7 percent of the audits the black advanced farther in the hiring process, and in 5 percent only the black received a job offer.

Opportunities Denied—Outcomes of the Hiring Process

The ultimate indicator of success in the job application process is, of course, a job offer. But no job seeker, however well qualified, can expect to receive an offer for every application he submits. Since auditors are competing against real applicants for every position, it is unreasonable to expect one or both to receive an offer in every case. In fact, only 33 percent of the audits culminated in job offers.[1]

A more useful measure of success, therefore, is how far into the hiring process an auditor was able to advance. Given their comparable characteristics and qualifications, both members of the audit teams should have had equal success in advancing through the application and interview stages, whether or not one or both ultimately received a job offer. When black applicants are unable to advance as far as equally qualified whites, they are effectively denied equal opportunities to compete for employment.

As reported in table 4.1, white applicants advanced farther in the hiring process than their black counterparts in 20 percent of the audits, whereas black auditors advanced farther than their white partners in 7 percent of the audits.[2] In other words, when a young black man applies for an entry-level position for which an equally qualified white candidate is also competing, there is a one in five chance that the black will be unable to advance as far in the process as an equally qualified white. Correspondingly, when a young white man applies for an entry-level position for which an equally qualified black candidate is also competing, there is a 7 percent chance that the white will be less successful than the black. Thus, given equally qualified white and black candidates, one white and the other black, if differential treatment occurs, it is three times more likely to favor the white than to favor the black.

In the majority of the cases where one auditor advanced further than his partner, he received a job offer whereas his partner did not. In 15 percent of the audits, only the white partner received a job offer (see table 4.2). This accounts for 75 percent of the cases where the white auditor advanced farther in the hiring process than his black counterpart.[3] The black auditor was the only member of the team to receive a

TABLE 4.1 Opportunity Denied: Who Advanced Farther in the Hiring Process? (percent of all completed audits)

	Percent	*t*-statistic
White advanced farther	20**	11.7
Black advanced farther	7**	4.5
Number of audits	438	

Note: ** indicates that percentage differs from zero at a 1 percent significance level.

TABLE 4.2 Opportunity Denied: Who Got a Job Offer? (percentage of all completed audits)

	Percent	*t*-statistic
Only white received offer	15**	7.0
Only black received offer	5**	4.1
Number of audits	438	

Note: ** indicates that percentage differs from zero at a 1 percent significance level.

job offer in 5 percent of the audits (71 percent of the cases in which the black auditor advanced further in the hiring process). Again, therefore, if an equally qualified white and black are in competition, differential treatment is three times more likely to favor the white than to favor the black.

At what stage in the hiring process is differential treatment most likely to occur? As illustrated by table 4.3, both black and white auditors were generally successful in submitting a job application; the incidence of unfavorable treatment at this initial stage was only 2 percent. Once beyond the application

TABLE 4.3   Opportunity Denied by Stage at which Unfavorable Treatment Occurred (percentage of audits with both partners remaining at that stage)

	Percent	t-statistic
Application		
White favored	2*	2.42
Black favored	0	—[a]
Number of audits	476	
Interview		
White favored	9**	7.45
Black favored	3**	4.33
Number of audits	465	
Job Offer		
White favored	8**	4.25
Black favored	4**	4.10
Number of audits	220	

Notes: ** indicates that percentage differs from zero at a 1 percent significance level. * indicates that percentage differs from zero at a 5 percent significance level.
a. Dash (—), not applicable.

stage, however, differential treatment was equally likely to occur at the formal interview stage or the job-offer stage. In 9 percent of the audits where both partners submitted an application, only the white partner received a formal interview (compared to 3 percent in which only the black was interviewed). And in 8 percent of the audits where both partners received a formal interview, only the white partner received a job offer (compared to only 4 percent in which only the black was offered a job).

There appears to be some variation in the prevalence of discrimination between labor markets. As shown in table 4.4, the incidence of unfavorable treatment toward blacks is

TABLE 4.4 Opportunity Denied by Metropolitan Area
(percent of all completed audits)

	Chicago	Washington, D.C.
Who advanced farther?		
White favored		
Percent	17**	23**
t-statistic	5.9	16.4
Black favored		
Percent	8*	7**
t-statistic	2.2	9.3
Who got a job offer?		
White favored		
Percent	10**	19**
t-statistic	3.8	11.0
Black favored		
Percent	5	6**
t-statistic	1.6	17.6
Number of audits	197	241

Note: ** indicates that percentage differs from zero at a 1 percent significance level. * indicates that percentage differs from zero at a 5 percent
significance level.

higher in Washington, D.C., than in Chicago. In Washington,
blacks face a 23 percent chance of being denied opportunities
to advance through the hiring process, compared to a 17
percent chance in Chicago. However, this difference is not
statistically significant at the 5 percent level. The share of
cases in which white auditors received a job offer but their
equally qualified black partners did not was 19 percent in
Washington compared to only 10 percent in Chicago, and this
difference is statistically significant at a 1 percent level. The
share of black-favored outcomes, does not differ between the
two metropolitan areas.

Opportunities Denied—Steering in the Hiring Process

In addition to being denied opportunities to advance through the hiring process, blacks were "steered" to less-desirable jobs than their white counterparts in a small but significant share of all audits, whether or not a job was actually offered. In some cases, blacks benefited from job steering. Overall, though, whites were slightly more likely to be favored than their black counterparts.

To document possible steering, the auditors were asked to indicate whether the jobs for which they were considered corresponded to the advertised positions for which they applied. When auditors reported that they were considered for a different job than the advertised position, they were asked to indicate whether this job was better, worse, or about the same as the advertised position. Wages, hours, and status were used in determining whether one job was better than another.

As an illustration, one audit team responded to an advertisement for sales personnel at a car dealership. The white auditor was considered for and offered a position in new car sales, whereas the black auditor was told that the only positions available were in used car sales. In another case, a team applied for an advertised position for a receptionist. The black was offered a job as a factory worker whereas the white was considered for the receptionist position. As illustrated by table 4.5, blacks were steered to less-desirable jobs than their white counterparts in 5 percent of the audits. Blacks were considered for more desirable jobs than their white partners in 3 percent of the audits. The same pattern of job steering occurred in both Chicago and Washington, although the incidence was higher for Washington.

TABLE 4.5   Differences in Job Quality (percentage of all completed audits)

	Chicago	Washington, D.C.	Total
White favored			
Percent	4**	5**	5**
t-statistic	7.9	7.9	9.4
Black favored			
Percent	2*	3*	3*
t-statistic	1.3	1.8	2.3
Number of audits	214	258	472

Note: ** indicates that percentage differs from zero at a 1 percent significance level. * indicates that percentage differs from zero at a 5 percent significance level.

Opportunities Diminished—Treatment in the Hiring Process

Even when both black and white job seekers advance to the same stage in the hiring process, one team member may be disadvantaged by discouraging treatment. For example, as indicated earlier, auditors may be discouraged from submitting an application, they may be required to wait long periods before being interviewed, or they may be given cursory interviews. Although these forms of unfavorable treatment do not *deny* a job seeker the opportunity to compete for a job, they may *diminish* his chances of success. Moreover, since finding a job often requires the submission of many applications, the cumulative effect of opportunity-diminishing treatment may be profoundly discouraging to a young job seeker. This section focuses on the extent to which black and white auditors were treated differently at the application and formal interview stage.[4] At each of these stages in the hiring process, the experiences of white and black auditors are compared for the subset of cases in which both teammates reached that stage.

It is worthwhile to emphasize at this point the importance placed on recording incidents of discouraging treatment consistently and objectively. As each stage in the hiring process was completed, auditors recorded their experiences on a structured data collection form. Members of each audit team were instructed to fill out the form immediately upon leaving an employer's office, prior to talking to one another or comparing notes. In addition, auditors were instructed to write down verbatim any positive or negative comments, any derogatory remarks, or any statements that they felt had racial implications. Audit supervisors reviewed the data collection instruments on a daily basis, and referred to the verbatim remarks whenever any questions of interpretation arose.

The Application Stage

In 98 percent of the audits, both the black and white auditors were successful in submitting applications for an advertised job. The auditors' treatment at this stage differed in two key respects: difficulty in applying and positive comments.[5]

As an illustration, in one audit the black auditor was asked several questions about his qualifications before receiving an application form, whereas his white counterpart was simply handed the form as a matter of routine. In other words, the minority job seeker experienced more difficulty than his white partner in submitting an application for the job. In another audit, the white partner reported the following positive comments about his chances for getting the job: "You are just what we are looking for.... We need more of us here.... As you can see, there are a lot of blacks who work here and we need to even the sides."

Auditors also indicated whether they received negative comments, they recorded the length of time they had to wait, and they reported if they were required to provide proof of identification, take a basic skills test, or submit other documents. However, no significant differences in treatment were discerned for these treatment measures.

Table 4.6 summarizes the incidence of discouraging treatment at the application stage for Chicago and Washington, D.C. Because patterns in the two metropolitan areas differed markedly, pooled results are not particularly meaningful. In Washington, black applicants encountered less favorable treatment than their white partners at the application stage in a substantial share of cases. Specifically, in 8 percent of the Washington audits, the black auditor experienced more difficulty than his white partner in obtaining an application, and in 6 percent of the audits, the white partner received more favorable comments. Altogether, black applicants were treated less favorably at the application stage than their white counterparts in 13 percent of the Washington audits.[6] Blacks were treated more favorably than their white counterparts in 3 percent of the Washington audits.

In Chicago, on the other hand, there is no evidence that white applicants were systematically favored over blacks at the application stage. In fact, blacks appear to have been given more encouragement in 14 percent of the audits, while whites were treated more favorably in 9 percent of the audits. In other words, when differential treatment occurs as part of the application stage in Chicago, it is actually more likely to favor the black candidate than the white candidate.

The Interview Stage

In 45 percent of the audits, both the black and the white auditors were successful in obtaining formal job interviews.[7] Table 4.7 demonstrates that in half of these cases, the black applicant was treated less favorably than his white counter-

TABLE 4.6 Differential Treatment at the Application Stage by Metropolitan Area (percentage of audits where both submited applications)

	Chicago	Washington, D.C.	Total
Difficulty in Applying			
White favored			
Percent	3*	8*	6*
t-statistic	2.3	2.0	2.7
Black Favored			
Percent	4**	2**	3**
t-statistic	3.1	3.2	3.9
Positive Comments			
White favored			
Percent	6*	6*	6**
t-statistic	2.4	2.0	3.2
Black Favored			
Percent	10**	2*	6*
t-statistic	2.9	2.1	2.5
Composite Index			
White favored			
Percent	9**	13**	10**
t-statistic	4.6	3.3	5.0
Black Favored			
Percent	14**	3*	8**
t-statistic	4.1	2.4	3.3
Number of Audits	214	251	465

Note: ** indicates that percentage differs from zero at a 1 percent significance level. * indicates that percentage differs from zero at a 5 percent significance level.

TABLE 4.7 Differential Treatment at the Formal Interview Stage by Metropolitan Area (percentage of audits where both received a formal interview)

	Chicago	Washington, D.C.	Total
Waiting Time			
White favored			
Percent	42**	32**	36**
t-statistic	5.9	4.5	7.2
Black Favored			
Percent	21**	17*	19**
t-statistic	3.3	2.6	4.3
Length of Interview			
White favored			
Percent	28**	50**	40**
t-statistic	4.2	5.8	6.4
Black Favored			
Percent	29**	22**	25**
t-statistic	4.2	2.3	4.3
Number of Interviewers			
White favored			
Percent	7**	7**	7**
t-statistic	3.2	4.1	5.5
Black Favored			
Percent	7**	2*	4**
t-statistic	4.5	2.5	3.9
Positive Comments			
White favored			
Percent	36**	43**	40**
t-statistic	4.1	3.6	5.5
Black Favored			
Percent	37**	13**	23**
t-statistic	4.6	2.9	4.1

(continued)

Table 4.7 *(continued)*

	Chicago	Washington, D.C.	Total
Negative Comments			
White favored			
Percent	11**	10**	10**
t-statistic	4.6	3.1	5.3
Black Favored			
Percent	18**	4*	10**
T-statistic	3.1	2.2	2.8
Composite Index			
White favored			
Percent	37**	60**	50**
t-statistic	3.4	7.1	6.8
Black Favored			
Percent	42**	16*	27**
t-statistic	5.2	2.2	4.0
Number of Audits	80	130	220

Note: ** indicates that percentage differs from zero at a 1 percent significance level. * indicates that percentage differs from zero at a 5 percent significance level.

part, whereas in 27 percent of the audits the black was treated more favorably.

Auditors were treated more or less favorably at the interview stage in five key respects: length of waiting time, length of interview, number of interviewers, positive comments, and negative comments.[8] As an illustration, when one black auditor responded to an ad for a blue collar job in an apartment complex, he was interviewed for 5 minutes and told to call back. In contrast, the white partner arrived next and was interviewed for 25 minutes. In another example, a black auditor reported that he had received a very discouraging impression of the job, including the statement that "your supervisor will work your butt off." The white partner, on the other hand, was told that the company offered great opportunities for advancement.

In over one-third of the audits in which both partners received an interview, the black partner had to wait at least five minutes longer than the white after arriving for his scheduled appointment, compared to 19 percent of the audits in which the white partner had to wait longer than the black. Black applicants were also more likely to receive shorter interviews; in 40 percent of the cases in which both applicants received an interview, the white auditor's interview was significantly longer. Again, however, the share of cases in which the black applicant was favored is considerable (25 percent). Consistent with the longer interview times, white applicants were interviewed by more people than their black counterparts in 7 percent of those audits where both received interviews, compared to 4 percent in which the black was interviewed by more people.

Whites were also more likely to receive encouraging comments during the interview than their black counterparts. In 40 percent of the audits where both partners received an interview, the white partner received more positive comments than his black counterpart, compared to 23 percent in which the black partner received more encouraging comments. Finally, both blacks and whites reported more discouraging comments than their partner in 10 percent of the cases where both were interviewed. Black applicants experienced less favorable treatment at the interview stage than their white counterparts in 50 percent of the audits in which both auditors received interviews. Black applicants received more favorable treatment than their white partners in 27 percent of such audits.

Patterns of unfavorable treatment in the interview process appear to differ significantly by location. In Washington, blacks who received interviews were treated less favorably than their white partners 60 percent of the time, compared to

16 percent of the time in which blacks were favored over whites. In Chicago, on the other hand, blacks who received interviews were actually slightly more likely to receive favorable treatment than their white counterparts. Thus, it is unclear whether differential treatment by the Chicago employers at the interview stage is random or systematically favors black applicants.

Variations in Patterns of Unfavorable Treatment

Results presented thus far indicate that black job seekers in both Chicago and Washington face a substantial probability of encountering unfavorable treatment. This section focuses on variations in audit outcomes in an attempt to determine what factors account for patterns of differential treatment. To sort out various influences on audit outcomes, we employed a statistical technique known as multinomial logit. This procedure makes it possible to estimate the independent impacts of auditor and employer characteristics on the probability that an employer will treat a black job applicant less favorably than a comparable white applicant. Specifically, we tested three hypotheses about patterns of unfavorable treatment in the employment process:

- Blacks are more likely to encounter unfavorable treatment in higher paying, higher status jobs and in jobs involving substantial customer contact.

- Blacks are more likely to encounter unfavorable treatment from white employers than from minority employers.

• Blacks are more likely to encounter unfavorable treatment when they apply for jobs in predominantly white neighborhoods.

A more complete explanation of the multinomial logit methodology is provided in appendix B.

In order to test the first hypothesis—regarding the impact of job type on the probability of unfavorable treatment—it was necessary to disentangle the independent differences in outcomes that occurred across audit teams. Appendix D presents the incidence of differential treatment for each of the ten audit teams. In Washington, all five teams experienced approximately the same incidence of white-favored and black-favored outcomes. In Chicago, there was considerable variation among teams in audit outcomes. These differences may be attributable partly to intangible differences among the teams or their behavior. However, it is highly likely that differences across teams are also related to differences in the types of jobs for which the teams applied. By design, audit teams were assigned to job openings for which they were most likely to appear qualified, given their experience and background. Consequently, if unfavorable treatment occurs more frequently in certain types of jobs, then the audit teams that applied for these jobs will appear to experience above average rates of differential treatment.

We estimated several models with job type and audit pairs separately and together in an attempt to sort out their independent effects. Advertised job openings were classified on the basis of both industry and occupation. Specifically, industry categories included (1) agriculture, forestry, fisheries, and mining; (2) construction; (3) manufacturing; (4) transportation, communication, and other public utilities; (5) wholesale and retail trade; (6) finance, banking, insurance, and real estate; (7) business services; (8) personal services; (9) hotels; and (10) restaurants. Occupational categories included (1) white collar; (2) sales and service; and (3) blue collar. Exploratory analysis indicated that differences in audit outcomes between Washington and Chicago persisted even after controlling for differences in the mix of audited firms and occupations. Therefore, we defined a series of categorical variables to group the audits according to metropolitan area, industry type, and occupation. To ensure sufficient numbers of observations in each group, some industries and occupations were combined with others that we considered similar in terms of job quality, job requirements and likely interaction with the public. Our underlying hypothesis was that unfavorable treatment of blacks was more likely in positions requiring higher skills or extensive interaction with the public, since prejudiced employers might believe that blacks are unqualified for high skilled positions or that customers would be averse to receiving services from black employees.

Both job type and audit pairs proved to have a significant effect in explaining the differential treatment. Appendix tables B-1 and B-2 report the logit coefficients for the job type and audit pair models when they were run separately. Both sets of variables have high *t*-statistics and a similar degree of overall explanatory power, as seen in the similar log likelihoods. If both sets of the variables are included in the estimating equation (as reported in appendix table B-3), the *t*-statistics of the individual variables become insignificant. But each set of variables as a whole was significant at the 1 percent level when added to the other set of variables, as seen in a likelihood ratio test of constrained and unconstrained models with each set of variables. In other words, there is sufficient evidence to suggest that both job categories and audit teams are important sources of variation in audit outcomes, but our data set simply does not contain enough observations to sort out the separate effects.

Because both sets of variables are measuring similar effects, and since we were extremely confident about the comparability of our audit teams and the consistency of their training, the job type variables seem to be the more likely source of most of the variation in audit outcomes. The evidence for the most part shows that blacks are much more likely to encounter unfavorable treatment in higher paying, higher status jobs and in jobs involving substantial customer contact. Table 4.8 summarizes the results of the multinomial logit analysis for the job type variables, reporting the probability for each job category that the white auditor advanced further in the hiring process than his equally qualified black partner. In general, unfavorable treatment is highest for white collar and sales and service jobs in Washington. Focusing on the eight job categories with above average probabilities of unfavorable treatment (over 20 percent), we find that six are in Washington, and six are white collar or sales and service positions. The highest incidence of unfavorable treatment, however, is for blue collar jobs in Washington retail firms.

Audit data from Chicago and Washington fail to provide conclusive evidence on the question of whether blacks are more likely to encounter unfavorable treatment from white employers than from minority employers. The best available indicator of the race of the employer was the race (or ethnicity) of the primary person conducting a formal interview. For audits in which neither applicant received a formal interview, the race of the employer could not reasonably be determined. Therefore, a dummy variable was introduced for the non-interview audits, so that the sample size would not have to be reduced. Appendix table B-4 presents the multinomial logit coefficients and summary statistics for this model. The addition of this group of variables is significant as a whole at the 1 percent level using a likelihood ratio test. However, none of the individual variables had significant *t*-statistics for the majority favored audits. It is not clear whether this significance of the group is due the race of the interviewer or that the audit did not get to the interview stage.

Most interviews (86 percent) were conducted by whites, with 11 percent conducted by blacks and 3 percent by other minorities. Eighteen percent of the audits with a black inter-

TABLE 4.8 Probability of Unfavorable Treatment by Job Category

Metropolitan Area	Industry Type	Occupation Type	Probability of Unfavorable Treatment
Washington, D.C.	Retail	Blue collar	30.0
Washington, D.C.	Retail	Sales and service	27.7
Washington, D.C.	Business and personal services	White collar, sales, and service	26.8
Washington, D.C.	Hotel	White collar, sales, and service	26.1
Washington, D.C.	Banking and real estate	Sales and service	24.8
Chicago	Restaurant	White collar, sales and service	22.6
Washington, D.C.	Restaurant	White collar, sales and service	22.6
Chicago	Retail, business, and personal services	Blue collar	21.1
Chicago	Retail	Sales and service	19.5
Chicago	Business and Personal	White collar, sales, and service	17.2
Washington, D.C.	Retail	White collar	15.6
Chicago	Hotel and Restaurant	Blue collar	13.8
Washington, D.C.	Business and personal services	Blue collar	13.4
Chicago	Hotel	White collar, sales, and service	13.3
Washington, D.C.	Hotel and restaurant	Blue collar	11.1
Chicago	Banking, retail, and real estate	White collar	0.0

Note: Probabilities are derived from a multinominal logit equation (table B-1). See appendix B for complete results.

viewer resulted in a white-favored outcome, compared to 19 percent of the audits with a white interviewer. It is worth noting that the incidence of *black*-favored outcomes was higher for audits with a black interviewer (27 percent) than for audits with a white interviewer (10 percent). In the multinomial logit equations, which attempted to quantify the role of interviewer race holding other differences among audits constant, race of the interviewer was not significantly related to the probability of a white-favored outcome. Receiving an interview from a black does, however, significantly increase the probability of a black-favored outcome. Thus, the evidence from these audits neither proves nor disproves the hypothesis that white employers are more likely than blacks to discriminate.

Finally, multinomial logit analysis does not support the hypothesis that blacks are more likely to encounter unfavorable treatment when they apply for jobs in predominantly white neighborhoods. Auditors recorded the address of the jobs to which they applied. These addresses were subsequently matched to Census tract identifiers, and to the estimated 1988 percentage black population in each Census tract.[9] Most of the audited jobs (62 percent) were located in tracts with less than 10 percent black population, with 29 percent located in tracts between 10 and 60 percent black, and only 9 percent in tracts with more than 60 percent black population.

A simpler variable, indicating only whether the employer was located in the central city or suburbs, was also tested. Appendix tables B-5 and B-6 report the logit models that include percent black and suburban location. A likelihood ratio test on models incorporating these variables showed that neither was significant at the 5 percent level. In other words, black job seekers in Washington and Chicago are no more likely to encounter discrimination from suburban employers than from similar firms (advertising similar positions) in the central city.

Black-White and Hispanic-Anglo Results

How does the experience of black and white job applicants in Washington, D.C., and Chicago compare to the experience of Hispanics and Anglos in The Urban Institute's earlier audit study, conducted in Chicago and San Diego in 1989? Table 4.9 summarizes key results of the two studies. In general, blacks appear less likely than Hispanics to be denied equal opportunity for advancement through the hiring process, but more likely than Hispanics to be denied a job that is offered to a comparable white Anglo applicant. In 31 percent of the Hispanic-Anglo employment audits, the majority partner advanced farther through the hiring process, compared to 20 percent of the black-white audits. These differences in results are statistically significant at the 1 percent significance level.

Hispanics were much more likely to experience unfavorable treatment at the application and interview stages than were blacks. At the application stage, the incidence of unfavorable treatment of Hispanics was 6 percent (compared to 2 percent for blacks), and at the interview stage, the incidence of unfavorable treatment of Hispanics was 18 percent (compared to 7 percent for blacks).

There are three possible explanations for the differences in results for blacks and Hispanics. First, in the Hispanic-Anglo audits, employers could identify Hispanic applicants by their accents during the initial telephone contact. Therefore, Hispanics could be denied the opportunity to apply even before visiting the employer in person. Black and white auditors could be less reliably distinguished over the telephone. Therefore, in the black-white audits, the audit did not officially begin (and differences in treatment did not begin being recorded) until the first contact in person.

This explanation certainly accounts for some of the difference between black-white and Hispanic-Anglo audit results.

TABLE 4.9   Results from Two Employment Audit Studies
(percentage of all audits completed)

	Total Black-White	Total Hispanic-Anglo
Who advanced farther?		
Majority favored	20	31
Minority favored	7	11
Who got a job offer?		
Majority favored	15	22
Minority favored	5	8

In 98 percent of the black-white audits, both partners were successful in submitting applications. In the Hispanic-Anglo audits, on the other hand, Hispanics were denied the opportunity to apply 9 percent of the time.[10] This finding suggests that, once a job seeker presents himself in person, he is likely to be able to submit an application for a job. Moreover, if employers can distinguish between minority and majority applicants over the telephone, minorities may be more likely to be denied the opportunity even to apply for job openings.

A second possible explanation for differences between the results of the black-white and Hispanic-Anglo audit studies is that, since blacks have historically initiated more challenges than Hispanics to discriminatory treatment (in employment and in other areas as well), employers may be more sensitive to the need to give the appearance of equal treatment to blacks, even though they are more likely to deny black applicants jobs for which they are qualified. Finally, it is possible that concern about documentation requirements required under the Immigration Reform and Control Act (IRCA) may have made some employers more resistant to even considering Hispanics for job openings than they were to considering blacks.

Notes, chapter 4

1. The rate was lower in Chicago (24 percent), where the job market was soft, and higher in Washington, D.C. (40 percent).

2. The t-statistics in this and subsequent tables test whether the observed incidences of unfavorable treatment are significantly different from zero. See appendix A for complete details.

3. In the remaining cases, the white auditor advanced farther but still received no job offer.

4. Auditors also recorded their treatment when they made follow-up calls to prospective employers, after submitting applications, and after formal interviews. Analysis of treatment in these telephone contacts yielded no significant evidence of differential treatment.

5. See appendix C for the precise definition of these treatment variables.

6. For this composite treatment index, an audit is classified as "no different" if auditors were treated equally on both the individual treatment indicators, or if one auditor was favored on one indicator while the other auditor was favored on the other indicator. Audits are classified as "white favored" if the white auditor was favored on both individual indicators, or if the white was favored on one and the black was not favored at all.

7. A formal interview was defined as a conversation between the applicant and a representative of the employer, in which at least one of the two parties was seated. This definition was imposed to distinguish between formal interviews and informal interactions (by telephone or in person) between applicants and prospective employers.

8. See appendix C for the precise definition of these treatment variables.

9. Estimated 1988 Census Tract characteristics were obtained from National Decision Systems, Encinitas, California.

10. Cross et al. (1990), table 5.1.

5

Summary and Conclusions

The Urban Institute's hiring audit study demonstrates that unequal treatment of black job seekers is entrenched and widespread.[1] The research contradicts claims that hiring practices today either favor blacks systematically or are effectively color-blind. In the Washington, D.C., and Chicago metropolitan areas, blacks receive unfavorable differential treatment 20 percent of the time they compete against comparable whites for entry-level positions. In contrast, whites receive unfavorable differential treatment 7 percent of the time they compete against comparably qualified blacks.

Over the last 25 years, black men have gained substantial ground relative to white men with regard to wages, income, and access to managerial positions. However, almost no progress has been made in labor force participation and unemployment rates. Indeed, recent trends show a widening gap between blacks and whites on these indicators. Arguments about reasons for this trend are not supported by systematic evidence, since most research on discrimination in employment has focused on relative wage rates, and little is known about either the extent or character of discriminatory hiring practices.

The Urban Institute, sponsored by the Rockefeller Foundation, has conducted the first study to directly measure differential treatment of white and black job seekers applying for entry-level employment. The study employed the "audit" methodology, which has been used extensively for over a decade to test for discrimination in housing, and was pioneered in the employment context by a 1989 Urban Institute study of discrimination against Hispanic job seekers. In the current hiring audit, 10 pairs of young men—each pair consisting of a black and a white—were carefully matched on all characteristics that could affect a hiring decision, and were trained to behave as similarly as possible in an interview setting. They applied in turn for entry-level jobs (requiring no special skills, experience, or training) advertised in the newspaper, and each applicant reported his treatment at every stage of the hiring process. Since both applicants were the same with respect to job qualifications, experience, and demeanor, systematic differences in treatment by employers can only be attributable to race. This methodology effectively catches employers in the act of discriminating.

A total of 476 hiring audits were conducted in the metropolitan areas of Washington, D.C., and Chicago during summer 1990. In one out of five audits, the white applicant was able to advance farther through the hiring process than his equally qualified black counterpart. In other words, the white was able to either submit an application, receive a formal interview, or be offered a job when the black was not. Overall, in one out of seven, or 15 percent, of the audits, the white was offered a job although his equally qualified black partner was not.[2]

In contrast, black auditors advanced farther than their white counterparts on only 7 percent of the audits, and the black auditors received job offers whereas their white partners did not in 5 percent of the audits. In sum, if equally qualified black and white candidates are competing for a job, differential treatment, when it occurs, is three times more likely to favor the white applicant than the black.

These results show that despite extensive legislative and regulatory protections and incentives to hire minorities, unfavorable treatment of young black men is widespread and pervasive across firms offering entry-level jobs in the Washington, D.C., and Chicago metropolitan areas. Moreover, the audit results indicate that reverse discrimination—favoring a black applicant over an equally qualified white—is far less common.

The hiring audit results should be viewed as realistic estimates of the incidence of discrimination in the two metropolitan areas we studied, for three reasons. First, the reported measures of differential treatment focus on outcomes of the hiring process, and do not include instances of discouraging treatment (negative comments, longer waits for scheduled appointments, cursory interviews), which were experienced by black applicants in as many as half the audits. Second, the job openings for which black and white auditors applied were selected from the classified advertisements of major metropolitan newspapers, and discrimination is presumably lower for advertised positions than for positions filled by less-public mechanisms, such as word of mouth, postings at the job site, or use of recruiters or employment agencies. Finally, all of the auditors participating in this study were actually college students who were overqualified for the positions for which they applied; they were articulate and poised, spoke and dressed conventionally, and posed as having had prior job experience. One would expect both blacks and whites with these characteristics to appear as exceptionally attractive candidates to prospective employers. In particular, the qualifications of the black auditors were substantially higher than those of the average black applicant for entry-level jobs.

Results from The Urban Institute's earlier audit study of discrimination against Hispanic job seekers, conducted in

Chicago and San Diego, indicate that Hispanics appear even more likely than blacks to be denied equal opportunity for advancement through the hiring process. Specifically, in 31 percent of the Hispanic-Anglo audits, the majority applicant advanced farther through the hiring process, compared to 20 percent of the black-white audits.

Overall levels of discrimination differed between the two metropolitan areas we studied. Despite the presence of the federal government with its long-standing equal opportunity policies, the incidence of unfavorable treatment was substantially higher in Washington than in Chicago. Specifically, whites advanced farther than their black counterparts 23 percent of the time in Washington, D.C., compared to 17 percent of the time in Chicago. And whites were offered jobs but their black partners were not in 19 percent of the Washington audits, compared to 10 percent of the Chicago audits. Outcomes favoring the black partner occurred at approximately the same rate in the two labor markets.

The likelihood of discrimination against blacks was not found to vary substantially between central city and suburban locations; blacks are no more likely to encounter unfavorable treatment by employers in suburban (and predominantly white) locations than in central city (and predominantly black) locations. This evidence contradicts the view that blacks encounter more discrimination when they seek employment in the suburbs, although it is important to keep in mind that only firms advertising available positions in the metropolitan newspaper were included in the audit study.

The type of job for which a minority applies proves to be the most important predictor of the likelihood of discrimination. In general, minorities are more likely to encounter discrimination in entry-level clerical jobs and in jobs involving client sales and service than in blue collar positions. Of the eight job categories with above-average levels of discrimination, six are in clerical or sales and service positions. In other words, discrimination against blacks appears to be highest in the types of jobs offering the highest wages and future income potential.

The fact that black job seekers in Washington, D.C., and Chicago were unable to advance as far in the hiring process as equally qualified whites in one out of five audits indicates that unfavorable treatment of black job seekers is widespread, and that discrimination contributes to black male unemployment and nonparticipation in the labor force. The results also contradict the view that reverse discrimination is commonplace. Evidence from hiring audits indicates that pressures to dismantle the machinery of civil rights enforcement are premature. Indeed, the prevalence of disparate treatment in the hiring process means that greater efforts are needed to detect discrimination and to provide victims with access to justice.

These results argue for a shift in the allocation of enforcement resources. In the years after the passage of the Civil Rights Act in 1964, enforcement resources—as measured by charges brought before the Equal Employment Opportunity Commission and employment discrimination cases—showed marked shift from hiring incidences to terminations (Donohue and Siegelman 1991:46). Our finding of substantial discrimination in hiring indicates a need to reverse this trend.

The Urban Institute has now completed two exploratory audit studies of hiring practices, each focusing on two metropolitan areas. These studies confirm that the audit methodology can be successfully adapted to test for differential treatment in employment. So long as close supervision of auditors is maintained by field managers, the audit methodology can generate concrete, probative evidence of differential outcomes on the basis of race or ethnicity. And, at least for entry-level job openings, the audit process need not be excessively intrusive.

Thus, the experimental phase in the development of the hiring audit methodology can be considered complete. Enforcement agencies should begin experimenting with testing to identify cases of hiring discrimination and to use the evidence developed in tests as a basis for litigation. Moreover, a logical next step is to design and implement a nationwide employment audit for both blacks and Hispanics. Like the national fair housing audit studies sponsored by the U.S. Department of Housing and Urban Development in 1977 and again in 1989, a full-scale hiring audit would provide statistically reliable estimates of the incidence of discrimination for the nation as a whole.

Notes, chapter 5

1. Use of the term "widespread" to describe the extent of discrimination found in this study derives from prior legal analysis and application of the term by the General Accounting Office (GAO) of the U.S. Specifically, the 1986 Immigration Reform and Control Act (IRCA) calls for the initiation of a process that could lead to the termination of the employer sanctions authorized by IRCA if the GAO were to find that sanctions had led to a "widespread pattern of discrimination" against eligible workers (Immigration and Naturalization Act, Section 274A(1)(1)(A)). After extensive analysis of IRCA's legislative history as well as U.S. civil rights legislation, the GAO determined that a "widespread pattern of discrimination" exists if there is a "serious pattern" and more than just a "few isolated cases of discrimination" (GAO, Immigration Reform; Employers Sanctions and the Question of Discrimination; GAO/GGD 90-62, March 1990). In the case of IRCA, the Comptroller General concluded that the introduction of discriminatory practices by 10 percent of all employers should be termed "widespread" for the purposes of the act. This level of discrimination is roughly half that found in this report.

2. All statistical results presented in this summary are significant at the 99-percent confidence level.

APPENDICES

APPENDIX A
Statistical Measures of the Incidence of Unfavorable Treatment

The calculation of the incidence of discrimination is based on a variable, say P, that equals one if the minority auditor encounters unfavorable treatment and zero otherwise. The share of audits in which the minority auditor encounters unfavorable treatment is equivalent to the average of P for all audits, which we will refer to as P^*. We calculate P^* as follows:

$$P^* = \frac{\sum\limits_{i=1}^{M} \sum\limits_{j=1}^{N_i} P_{ij}}{\sum\limits_{i=1}^{M} N_i} \tag{A.1}$$

where P_{ij} is the result of the jth audit for pair i; N_i is the number of audits completed by pair i, and M is the number of pairs.

The next step is to determine whether the incidence of unfavorable treatment could have occurred by chance. That is, we must test the null hypothesis $P^* = \dot{0}$. This hypothesis can be tested by using the t-statistic, which is formed by dividing P^* by its standard error. Because the Employment Discrimination Study (EDS) audits are "clustered" by auditor pairs, however, applying the usual formula for the standard error to P, which is appropriate for a simple, unclustered random sample, understates the true standard error, and, hence, overstates (in absolute value) the t-statistic.

The impact of the clustered sample design on the standard error, known as the "design effect," is discussed in most statistics texts (e.g., Cochran 1977). We use the following formula for the variance, which adjusts for clustering in the sample:

$$\sigma^2_{p*} = \frac{\sum\limits_{j=1}^{M} w_i \, (P_i^* - P^*)^2}{(M-1)}, \qquad (A.2)$$

where

$$P_i^* = \frac{\sum\limits_{j=1}^{N_i} P_{ij}}{N_i}$$

and

$$w_i = \frac{N_i}{\sum\limits_{i=1}^{M} N_i}$$

This approach corresponds to the "ultimate cluster estimate" of the variance defined in Hansen, Hurwitz, and Madow (1953a). It can be shown that this formula can be rewritten as a function of both the within-pair variation and the between-pair variation in P (Hansen, Hurwitz, and Mandow 1953b; Kish 1965). To give appropriate weight to each pair in the overall variance, the squared deviations are weighted by N_i, the number of audits completed by the pair. The t-statistic is calculated by dividing P^* by the standard error, σ, which is obtained by taking the square root of the variance given by (A.2). These t-statistics will have $M-1$ degrees of freedom. In the EDS there were five pairs in each city, so $M-1 = 4$ and the null hypothesis, $P^* = 0$, may be rejected at the 95 percent confidence level if P^*/σ is greater than 2.78. Rejecting the null hypothesis is equivalent to saying that one accepts the hypothesis that the observed incidence of unfavorable treatment does not differ from zero simply by chance.

We conclude by noting that the weighted variance in (A.2) is consistent with the use of the unweighted mean in (A.1) because, in this case, the weighted and unweighted means are identical. This can be shown by expanding the weighted mean P_w^*:

$$P_w^* = \sum_{i=1}^{M} w_i P_i^* = \frac{\sum_{i=1}^{M} N_i \dfrac{\sum_{j=1}^{N_i} P_{ij}}{N_i}}{\sum_{i=1}^{M} N_i} = \frac{\sum_{i=1}^{M} \sum_{j=1}^{N_i} P_{ij}}{\sum_{i=1}^{M} N_i} = P.^* \qquad (A.3)$$

Appendix B
Multivariate Analysis of Discrete Choice in Hiring Audits

Estimates of the incidence of unfavorable treatment of auditors build on a simple distinction made by most other fair housing and employment audit studies. For any variable measuring the way an auditor was treated, an audit can be classified as "white-favored," "black-favored," or "neutral." Consider, for example, the variable indicating whether the auditor received a formal interview. If the white auditor was told yes and the black auditor was told no, then the audit is classified as "white favored." If both auditors were told yes or both were told no, the audit is classified as neutral. And if the black auditor was told yes and the white auditor was told no, then the audit is classified as "black favored."

The three categories in this classification scheme can be interpreted as the choices an employer can make. That is, an employer can decide to favor white applicants, to favor black applicants, or to treat all applicants the same. Methods for studying this type of choice situation, in which a decision maker selects one of a discrete number of choices, are widely used in economics. For example, discrete choice models have been used to investigate the decision to own or rent, to drive or take the bus, and to participate or not in the labor force. A discrete choice model can be directly applied to the choices in an employment audit classification scheme.

The great advantage of discrete choice models is that they have a clear behavioral foundation. To be specific, these models assume that the utility, or satisfaction, an employer receives for each choice can be described by a utility index, U, which consists of a deterministic component, V, and a random component, e. Thus, for a given employer and the ith choice, the utility index is:

$$U_i = V_i + e_i. \tag{B.1}$$

In the case of hiring audits, V_i is a function of audit attributes, such as the characteristics of the employer, the advertised position, and the auditor. In contrast, e_i is a function of random events, such as the employer's mood or how close the interview is to lunchtime, which could favor either the white or the black auditor. A rational employer selects the choice that maximizes his or her utility; that is, the employer picks the choice with the highest utility index.

This framework makes it clear that an employer's choice depends on both the systematic factors that influence the Vs and on the distribution of the random error terms, the es. A large positive random error for one choice, for example, could lead an employer to make that choice even if the systematic factors favored a different one. By combining a specification for systematic utility as a function of the explanatory variables with an assumption about the distribution of the error term, one can derive expressions for the probability that an employer will make a given choice and then estimate the extent to which systematic factors are at work.

To be more specific, we assume that the systematic component of utility is a linear function of observable employer, auditor, and job characteristics and that e follows the so-called extreme-value distribution. These assumptions lead to a particular form of the discrete choice model that economists call the multinomial logit model. For a detailed discussion of this model, see Judge et al. (1985) or Boersch-Supan (1987). With three choices, the logit probabilities can be written:

$$P_1 = \frac{exp. \left(\sum_j \beta_{1j} X_j\right)}{1 + exp. \left(\sum_j \beta_{1j} X_j\right) + exp. \left(\sum_j \beta_{2j} X_j\right)}, \quad \text{(B.2)}$$

$$P_2 = \frac{exp. \left(\sum_j \beta_{2j} X_j\right)}{1 + exp. \left(\sum_j \beta_{1j} X_j\right) + exp. \left(\sum_j \beta_{2j} X_j\right)}, \quad \text{(B.3)}$$

and
$$P_3 = 1 - P_1 - P_2 \quad \text{(B.4)}$$

Using well-known statistical procedures, called maximum-likelihood estimation, the coefficients in these equations, the βs, can be estimated.

Note that multinomial logit models require an equation for every choice except one. The probability of the remaining choice can then be determined by the requirement that the probabilities of the choices must add up to one. It follows that the number of coefficients to be estimated is $(M-1) J$, where M is the number of choices and J is the number of explanatory variables. The cases considered here all involve three choices, namely to favor the white auditor, to favor the black auditor, or to be neutral. With three choices, the number of estimated parameters is twice the number of explanatory variables. For the multinomial regression results of the Employment Discrimination Study, see tables B-1 through B-6.

TABLE B-1 Multinomial Logistic Model for Outcomes of Employment Audits:
1. No Difference 2. White Favored 3. Black Favored

Industry Type	Occupation Type	White Favored (vs. No Difference)	Black Favored (vs. No Difference)
Chicago			
Retail	Sales and service	-1.25**	-1.76**
		(0.36)	(0.44)
Banking and retail	White collar	-12.67	-1.70
		(170.01)	(0.77)
Business and personal service	White collar, sales, and service	-1.45**	-2.83**
		(0.56)	(1.02)
Retail, business, and personal services	Blue collar	-1.32*	-2.01**
		(0.56)	(0.75)
Hotel	White collar, sales, and service	-1.79*	-12.70
		(0.76)	(165.58)
Restaurant	White collar, sales, and service	-1.19**	-2.40**
		(0.36)	(0.60)
Hotel and restaurant	Blue collar	-1.83**	-3.21**
		(0.54)	(1.02)

(continued)

Table B-1 *(continued)*

Industry Type	Occupation Type	White Favored (vs. No Difference)	Black Favored (vs. No Difference)
Washington, D.C.			
Retail	White collar	-1.66** (0.55)	-12.65 (121.88)
Retail	Sales and service	-0.88** (0.34)	-3.36** (1.01)
Retail	Blue collar	-0.69 (0.50)	-2.48* (1.04)
Banking and real estate	Sales and service	-0.87 (0.53)	-1.79* (0.76)
Business and personal services	White collar, sales, and service	-0.92 (0.48)	-1.32* (0.56)
Business and personal services	Blue collar	-1.66** (0.55)	-2.35** (0.74)
Hotel	White collar, sales, and service	-1.04* (0.47)	-1.45 (0.56)
Restaurant	White collar, sales, and service	-1.15* (0.47)	-12.40 (112.87)
Hotel and restaurant	Blue collar	-1.39** (0.46)	-2.48 (0.74)
Log likelihood -309.78		*Number of observations* 438	

Note: Numbers in parentheses are standard errors. * significant at the 5 percent level. ** significant at the 1 percent level.

TABLE B-2 Multinomial Logistic Model for Outcomes of Employment Audits: 1. No Difference 2. White Favored 3. Black Favored

Attributes	White Favored (vs. No Difference)	Black Favored (vs. No Difference)
Chicago		
Auditor pair 1	-0.79 (0.38)	-1.99** (0.62)
Auditor pair 2	-1.50** (0.45)	-1.35** (0.42)
Auditor pair 3	-1.92** (0.48)	-1.92** (0.48)
Auditor pair 4	-1.42** (0.42)	-12.58 (99.95)
Auditor pair 5	-1.79** (0.44)	-12.74 (97.19)
Washington, D.C.		
Auditor pair 1	-0.92** (0.34)	-2.01** (0.53)
Auditor pair 2	-0.97** (0.31)	-2.51** (0.60)
Auditor pair 3	-1.24** (0.31)	-2.42** (0.52)
Auditor pair 4	-1.35** (0.42)	-2.20** (0.61)
Auditor pair 5	-1.24** (0.38)	-2.74** (0.73)

Log likelihood -312.82   *Number of observations 438*

Note: Numbers in parentheses are standard errors. * significant at the 5 percent level. ** significant at the 1 percent level.

TABLE B-3 Multinomial Logistic Model for Outcomes of Employment Audits:
1. No Difference 2. White Favored 3. Black Favored

Industry Type	Occupation Type	White Favored (vs. No Difference)	Black Favored (vs. No Difference)
Chicago			
Retail	Sales and service	-0.39 (0.55)	-1.05 (0.80)
Banking and retail	White collar	-11.97 (174.63)	-1.78 (1.02)
Business and personal service	White collar, sales, and service	-0.53 (0.74)	-2.41 (1.31)
Retail, business, and personal services	Blue collar	-0.53 (0.71)	-1.73 (1.06)
Hotel	White collar, sales, and service	-1.02 (0.85)	-12.17 (155.91)
Restaurant	White collar, sales, and service	-0.64 (0.45)	-2.01** (0.75)
Hotel and restaurant	Blue collar	-1.20 (0.67)	-3.51** (1.25)
Auditor pair 2		-0.62 (0.64)	0.89 (0.83)

Auditor pair 3		-1.12 (0.66)	-0.20 (0.86)
Auditor pair 4		-0.87 (0.62)	-10.93 (100.38)
Auditor pair 5		-1.13 (0.61)	-10.87 (94.54)
Washington, D.C.			
Retail	White collar	-1.43* (0.61)	-12.31 (127.05)
Retail	Sales and service	-0.66 (0.46)	-2.91** (1.11)
Retail	Blue collar	-0.48 (0.62)	-1.94 (1.19)
Banking and real estate	Sales and service	-0.65 (0.62)	-1.34 (0.92)
Business and personal services	White collar, sales, and service	-0.71 (0.59)	-0.67 (0.77)
Business and personal services	Blue collar	-1.46* (0.70)	-1.75 (1.02)

(continued)

Table B-3(continued)

Industry Type	Occupation Type	White Favored (vs. No Difference)	Black Favored (vs. No Difference)
Hotel	White collar, sales, and service	-0.93 (0.58)	-0.93 (0.73)
Restaurant	White collar, sales, and service	-1.04 (0.55)	-12.09 (116.76)
Hotel and restaurant	Blue collar	-1.25* (0.59)	-1.80 (0.94)
Auditor pair 2		0.01 (0.48)	-0.92 (0.84)
Auditor pair 3		-0.22 (0.52)	-0.62 (0.85)
Auditor pair 4		-0.46 (0.55)	-0.23 (0.86)
Auditor pair 5		-0.36 (0.53)	-1.07 (0.96)

Log likelihood   -296.24   *Number of observations*   438

Note: Numbers in parentheses are standard errors. * significant at the 5 percent level. ** significant at the 1 percent level.

TABLE B-4 Multinomial Logistic Model for Outcomes of Employment Audits: 1. No Difference 2. White Favored 3. Black Favored

Industry Type	Occupation Type	White Favored (vs. No Difference)	Black Favored (vs. No Difference)
Chicago			
Retail	Sales and service	-1.36**	-1.27**
		(0.39)	(0.47)
Banking and retail	White collar	-12.77	-1.03
		(169.03)	(0.84)
Business and personal service	White collar, sales, and service	-1.53**	-2.99**
		(0.57)	(1.10)
Retail, business, and personal services	Blue collar	-1.43*	-1.33
		(0.59)	(0.80)
Hotel	White collar, sales, and service	-1.92*	-11.53
		(0.80)	(150.18)
Restaurant	White collar, sales, and service	-1.33**	-1.60*
		(0.40)	(0.63)
Hotel and restaurant	Blue collar	-1.98**	-2.24*
		(0.58)	(1.05)

(continued)

Table B-4 (continued)

Industry Type	Occupation Type	White Favored (vs. No Difference)	Black Favored (vs. No Difference)
Washington, D.C.			
Retail	White collar	-1.73** (0.56)	-12.17 (115.51)
Retail	Sales and service	-0.98** (0.37)	-3.23** (1.06)
Retail	Blue collar	-0.82 (0.53)	-1.76 (1.07)
Banking and real estate	Sales and service	-0.98 (0.58)	-2.17* (0.93)
Business and personal services	White collar, sales, and service	-0.92 (0.49)	-1.46* (0.60)
Business and personal services	Blue collar	-1.77** (0.58)	-2.21** (0.84)
Hotel	White collar, sales, and service	-1.20* (0.54)	-0.37 (0.73)
Restaurant	White collar, sales, and service	-1.26* (0.49)	-12.07 (101.25)
Hotel and restaurant	Blue collar	-1.53** (0.50)	-1.90* (0.84)

Other Attributes	White Favored (vs. No Difference)	Black Favored (vs. No Difference)
Black interviewer	0.14	1.58*
	(0.63)	(0.69)
Other race interviewer	-0.54	0.58
	(1.11)	(0.81)
Non interview audit	0.20	-2.10**
	(0.27)	(0.61)
Log likelihood -294.04	*Number of observations* 438	

Note: Numbers in parentheses are standard errors. * significant at the 5 percent level. ** significant at the 1 percent level.

TABLE B-5 Multinomial Logistic Model for Outcomes of Employment Audits:1. No Difference 2. White Favored 3. Black Favored

Industry Type	Occupation Type	White Favored (vs. No Difference)	Black Favored (vs. No Difference)
Chicago			
Retail	Sales and service	-1.25** (0.36)	-1.82** (0.45)
Banking and retail	White collar	-12.66 (169.08)	-1.74* (0.77)
Business and personal service	White collar, sales, and service	-1.44* (0.56)	-2.92** (1.04)
Retail, business, and personal services	Blue collar	-1.31* (0.57)	-2.12** (0.77)
Hotel	White collar, sales, and service	-1.77* (0.77)	-12.86 (164.07)
Restaurant	White collar, sales, and service	-1.15** (0.39)	-2.67** (0.66)
Hotel and restaurant	Blue collar	-1.82** (0.55)	-3.34** (1.03)

Washington, D.C.			
Retail	White collar	-1.64**	-12.80
		(0.55)	(120.05)
Retail	Sales and service	-0.85*	-3.58**
		(0.36)	(1.04)
Retail	Blue collar	-0.63	-2.85**
		(0.53)	(1.10)
Banking and real estate	Sales and service	-0.84	-2.06*
		(0.55)	(0.82)
Business and personal services	White collar, sales, and service	-0.88	-1.54*
		(0.50)	(0.60)
Business and personal services	Blue collar	-1.63**	-2.53**
		(0.55)	(0.76)
Hotel	White collar, sales, and service	-1.02*	-1.63**
		(0.49)	(0.60)
Restaurant	White collar, sales, and service	-1.15*	-12.48
		(0.48)	(111.91)
Hotel and restaurant	Blue collar	-1.38**	-2.57**
		(0.46)	(0.75)

(continued)

Table B-5 *(continued)*

Other Attributes	White Favored (vs. No Difference)	Black Favored (vs. No Difference)
Percent black in census tract of employment location	-0.00 (0.01)	0.01 (0.01)
Dummy for missing census tract data	0.08 (0.44)	-0.07 (0.79)
Log likelihood -308.94	*Number of observations*	438

Numbers in parentheses are standard errors. * significant at the 5 percent level. ** significant at the 1 percent level

TABLE B-6 Multinomial Logistic Model for Outcomes of Employment Audits: 1. No Difference
2. White Favored 3. Black Favored

Industry Type	Occupation Type	White Favored (vs. No Difference)	Black Favored (vs. No Difference)
Chicago			
Retail	Sales and service	-1.25**	-1.73**
		(0.37)	(0.46)
Banking and retail	White collar	-12.67	-1.68*
		(169.99)	(0.77)
Business and personal service	White collar, sales, and service	-1.45*	-2.79**
		(0.57)	(1.04)
Retail, business, and personal services	Blue collar	-1.33*	-1.97
		(0.58)	(0.77)
Hotel	White collar, sales, and service	-1.79*	-12.70
		(0.76)	(165.54)
Restaurant	White collar, sales, and service	-1.20**	-2.38**
		(0.36)	(0.61)
Hotel and restaurant	Blue collar	-1.83**	-3.21**
		(0.54)	(1.02)

(continued)

Table B-6 *(continued)*

Industry Type	Occupation Type	White Favored (vs. No Difference)	Black Favored (vs. No Difference)
Washington, D.C.			
Retail	White collar	-1.67** (0.59)	-12.56 (121.83)
Retail	Sales and service	-0.89* (0.41)	-3.27** (1.07)
Retail	Blue collar	-0.70 (0.57)	-2.37* (1.12)
Banking and real estate	Sales and service	-0.89 (0.59)	-1.70* (0.85)
Business and personal services	White collar, sales, and service	-0.93 (0.54)	-1.23* (0.66)
Business and personal services	Blue collar	-1.67** (0.59)	-2.26** (0.81)
Hotel	White collar, sales, and service	-1.05* (0.50)	-1.39 (0.60)
Restaurant	White collar, sales, and service	-1.16* (0.50)	-12.32 (112.81)
Hotel and restaurant	Blue collar	-1.39** (0.49)	-2.41** (0.78)

Other Attributes	White Favored (vs. No Difference)	Black Favored (vs. No Difference)
Suburban location of employer	.01 (0.29)	-0.12 (0.45)
Log likelihood	-308.94	Number of observations	438

Numbers in parentheses are standard errors. * significant at the 5 percent level. ** significant at the 1 percent level.

Appendix C
Definition of Treatment Variables at the Application and Interview Stages

In addition to measuring the incidence of unfavorable treatment that *denies* minorities the equal opportunity to compete for employment, this study measured treatment that may *discourage* minorities from pursuing a particular job prospect or from continuing a vigorous job search over the long term. For audits in which both partners were successful in submitting a formal application, we analyzed differences in treatment at the application stage, and for audits in which both partners received a formal interview, we analyzed differences in treatment at the interview stage.

Two treatment measures were used to document differential treatment at the application stage:

1. *Difficulty in applying*: Auditors reported whether they were (1) given an application form immediately upon request; (2) given an application after a few questions were asked; or (3) given the application only after many questions were asked and the auditor had made several requests to apply. If the black auditor had more difficulty

than his white partner in obtaining an application form, the audit was classified as "white favored," and if the white auditor had more difficulty, the audit was classified as "black favored." If both teammates experienced the same degree of difficulty, the audit was classified as "no difference."

2. *Positive comments*: Auditors indicated whether or not they received positive comments in five categories: the job, their qualifications, their chances of getting the job, their chances for advancement, their chances for job security. If the white auditor received positive comments in more categories than his black partner, the audit was classified as "white favored," and if the black auditor received positive comments in more categories, the audit was classified as "black favored." If both teammates reported positive comments in the same number of categories, the audit was classified as "no difference."

Five treatment measures were used to document differential treatment at the interview stage:

1. *Length of waiting time*: Auditors reported the time they had to wait after arriving (on time) for a scheduled interview appointment. The average waiting time across all audits was less than five minutes. Therefore, we concluded that a differential between black and white auditors of five minutes or more represented a meaningful difference in treatment. If the black auditor had to wait at least five minutes longer than his white partner after arriving for a scheduled interview appointment, the audit was classified as "white favored," and if the white auditor had to wait five or more minutes longer, the audit was classified as "black

favored." Audits in which the lengths of wait for the two teammates were within five minutes of one another were classified as "no difference."

2. *Length of interview:* Auditors recorded the amount of time they spent in a formal interview. The average interview time for all audits was less than 10 minutes, and we concluded that a difference of 5 minutes or more in interview time represented a meaningful difference in treatment. If the white auditor was interviewed for at least 5 minutes longer than his black partner, the audit was classified as "white favored," and if the black auditor was interviewed for 5 or more minutes longer, the audit was classified as "black favored." Audits in which the lengths of the interviews for each teammate were within 5 minutes of one another were classified as "no difference."

3. *Number of interviewers*: Auditors recorded the number of people who interviewed them formally. The modal value for this treatment variable was one, and we concluded that any differential in the number of interviewers represented a meaningful difference in treatment. If the white auditor was interviewed by more people than his black partner, the audit was classified as "white favored," and if the black auditor was interviewed by more people, the audit was classified as "black favored." Audits in which both teammates were interviewed by the same number of people were classified as "no difference."

4. *Positive comments*: Auditors indicated whether or not they received positive comments in five categories: the job, their qualifications, their chances of getting the job, their chances for advancement,

and their chances for job security. If the white auditor received positive comments in more categories than his black partner, the audit was classified as "white favored," and if the black auditor received positive comments in more categories, the audit was classified as "black favored." If both teammates reported positive comments in the same number of categories, the audit was classified as "no difference."

5. *Negative comments*: Auditors indicated whether or not they received negative comments in five categories: the job, their qualifications, their chances of getting the job, their chances for advancement, and their chances for job security. If the black auditor received negative comments in more categories than his white partner, the audit was classified as "white favored," and if the white auditor received negative comments in more categories, the audit was classified as "black favored." If both teammates reported negative comments in the same number of categories, the audit was classified as "no difference."

APPENDIX D
Audit Outcomes by Audit Pairs

Pair	Number of Audits	Audit Outcome (percentage)		
		No Difference	White Favored	Black Favored
Chicago				
Audit Pair 1	35	62.9	28.6	8.6
Audit Pair 2	40	67.5	15.0	17.5
Audit Pair 3	44	77.3	11.4	11.4
Audit Pair 4	36	80.6	19.4	0.0
Audit Pair 5	42	85.7	14.3	0.0
Washington, D.C.				
Audit Pair 1	46	65.2	26.1	8.7
Audit Pair 2	54	68.5	25.9	5.6
Audit Pair 3	62	72.6	21.0	6.5
Audit Pair 4	37	73.0	18.9	8.1
Audit Pair 5	42	73.8	21.4	4.8

References

Abraham, K. 1987. "Help-Wanted Advertising, Job Vacancies, and Unemployment." *Brookings Papers on Economics Activity* (1): 207-48.

Belton, R. 1990. "The Dismantling of the Griggs Disparate Impact Theory and the Future of Title VII: The Need for a Third Reconstruction." *Yale Law and Policy Review* 8:223.

Bendick, M., Jr. 1989. "Auditing Race Discrimination in Hiring: A Research Design." Washington, D.C.: Bendick and Egan Economic Consultants, Inc.

Bendick, Marc, Jr., and Mary Lou Egan. 1988. "JOBS: Employment Opportunities in the Washington Metropolitan Area for Persons with Limited Employment Qualification." Washington, D.C.: Greater Washington Research Center.

Boersch-Supan, Axel. 1987. *Econometric Analysis of Discrete Choice*. Lecture Notes in Mathematical Systems, no. 296, edited by M. Beckmann and W. Krelle. Berlin: Springer-Verlag.

Briggs, V. 1990. "Employer Sanctions and the Question of Discrimination: The GAO Study in Perspective." *International Migration Review* 24:803-15.

Carr, Oliver T., Jr., et al. 1988. *Opportunity Ladders: Can Area Employment Possibilities Improve the Prospects for Washingtonians in Long-Term Poverty?* Washington, D.C.: Greater Washington Research Center.

Cochran, W.G. 1977. *Sampling Techniques*, 3rd edition. New York: John Wiley and Sons.

Corcoran, Mary, Linda Datcher, and Greg Duncan. 1980. "Most Workers Find Jobs through Word of Mouth." *Monthly Labor Reviews* 103(8):33-35.

Cross, H., G. Kenney, J. Mell, and W. Zimmermann. 1990. *Employer Hiring Practices: Differential Treatment of Hispanic and Anglo Job Seekers*. Washington, D.C.: Urban Institute Press.

Donohue, J.J., and P. Siegelman. 1991. "The Changing Nature of Employment Discrimination Litigation." Draft. Chicago: Northwestern University School of Law.

Ellwood, D. 1986. "The Spatial Mismatch Hypothesis: Are There Teenage Jobs Missing in the Ghetto?" In *The Black Youth Employment Crisis*, edited by R. Freeman and H. Holzer. Chicago: University of Chicago Press.

Epstein, Richard A. 1990. "The Paradox of Civil Rights." *Yale Law and Policy Review* 8(2):299-319.

Fix, M., and F. Bean. 1990. "The Findings and Policy Implications of the GAO Report and The Urban

Institute Hiring Audit." *International Migration Review* 24:816-27.

Freeman, R. 1990. "Employment and Earnings of Disadvantaged Young Men in a Labor Shortage Economy." Working Paper 3444. Cambridge, Mass: National Bureau of Economic Research.

Gregory, Vikki L. 1988. "ET: Employment and Training Activities Serving Predominantly Low-Income Residents of Washington, D.C., with Limited Employment Qualifications." Washington, D.C.: Greater Washington Research Center.

Hansen, Morris M., William N. Hurwitz, and William G. Mandow. 1953a. *Sample Survey Methods and Applications*. Vol. 1. *Methods and Applications*. New York: John Wiley & Sons, Inc.

_____. 1953b. *Sample Survey Methods and Theory*. Vol. 2. *Theory*. New York: John Wiley & Sons, Inc.

Heckman, James J., and J. Hoult Verkerke. 1990. "Racial Disparity and Employment Discrimination Law: An Economic Perspective." *Yale Law and Policy Review* 8(2):276-99.

Holzer H. 1989. "The Spatial Mismatch Hypothesis: What Has the Evidence Shown?" Michigan State University Working Paper. Lansing: Michigan State University.

_____. 1988. "Search Methods Used by Unemployed Youth." *Journal of Labor Economics* 6(1): 1-20.

_____. 1987a. "Informal Job Search and Black Youth Unemployment." *American Economic Review* 77:446-52.

_____. 1987b. "Job Search by Employed and Unemployed Youth." *Industrial and Labor Relations Review* 40(4):601-11.

Ihlanfeldt, K. R., and D. L. Sioquist. 1990. "Job Accessibility and Racial Differences in Youth Employment Rates." *American Economic Review* 80(1):267-76.

_____. 1989. "The Impact of Job Decentralization on the Economic Welfare of Central City Blacks." *Journal of Urban Economics* 26:110-30.

Jaynes, G.D. 1990. "The Labor Market Status of Black Americans: 1939-1985." *Journal of Economic Perspectives* 4(4): 9-24.

Jencks, C., and S. Mayer. 1990. "Residential Segregation, Job Proximity, and Black Job Opportunities." In *Inner-City Poverty in the United States,* edited by L. Lynn, Jr., and M.G.H McGeary, 187-222. Washington, D.C.: National Academy Press.

Judge, George G., et al. 1985. *The Theory and Practice of Econometrics,* 2nd edition. New York: John Wiley and Sons.

Kirschenman, Joleen, and K.M. Neckerman. 1991. "We'd Love to Hire Them But . . .: The Meaning of Race for Employers." In *The Urban Underclass,* edited by Christopher Jencks and Paul E. Peterson. Washington, D.C.: Brookings Institution.

Kish, Leslie. 1965. *Survey Sampling.* New York: John Wiley & Sons, Inc.

Massey, D.S., and N.A. Denton. 1989. "Hypersegregation in U.S. Metropolitan Areas: Blacks and Hispanic Segregation Along Five Dimensions." *Demography* 26(3): 373-91.

Rees, A. 1986. "An Essay on Youth Joblessness." *Journal of Economic Literature* 24:613-28.

Reitz, J.G. 1988. "Less Racial Discrimination in Canada, or Simply Less Racial Conflict? Implications of Comparisons with Britain." *Canadian Public Policy* 14 (2):424-41.

Reuter, Peter, Robert MacCoun, Patrick Murphy, Allan Abrahamse, and Barbara Simon. 1990. *Money from Crime: A Study of the Economics of Drug Dealing in Washington, D.C.* Santa Monica, Calif.: RAND.

Schumann, H., C. Steeh and L. Bobo. 1985. *Racial Attitudes in America: Trends and Interpretations.* Cambridge, Mass.: Harvard University Press.

Smith, T.W. 1990. "Ethnic Images." General Social Sciences Topical Report 19. Chicago: National Opinion Research Corp.

Strauss, D.A. 1990. "The Law and Economics of Racial Discrimination in Employment." Paper presented at the Georgetown University Conference on the Law and Economics of Racial Discrimination in Employment, November 30, Washington, D.C.

Swoboda, F. 1990. "Workplace Discrimination Perceived as Prevalent." *Washington Post*, July 9, p. A12.

Turner, M. A., R. Struyk, and J. Yinger. 1991. *Housing Discrimination Study Synthesis.* Washington, D.C.: Urban Institute.

U.S. Bureau of the Census. 1990. *1987 Survey of Minority-Owned Business Enterprises: Black.* Publ. #MB87-1. Washington, D.C.: U.S. Government Printing Office.

U.S. Bureau of Labor Statistics. 1989a. Employment, Hours, and Earnings: States and Areas, 1972-87. Bulletin 2320, vols. 1, 2. Washington, D.C.: U.S. Government Printing Office.

_____. 1989b. *Geographic Profile of Employment and Unemployment.* Bulletin 2327. Washington, D.C.: U.S. Government Printing Office.

_____. 1989c. *Handbook of Labor Statistics.* Bulletin 2340. Washington, D.C.: U.S. Government Printing Office.

_____. 1988. Geographic Profile of Employment and Unemployment. Bulletin 2305. Washington, D.C.: U.S. Government Printing Office.

_____. 1987. *Geographic Profile of Employment and Unemployment.* Bulletin 2279. Washington, D.C.: U.S. Government Printing Office

Wielgosz, J., and S. Carpenter. 1987. "The Effectiveness of Alternative Methods of Searching for Jobs and Finding Them: An Exploratory Analysis of Data Bearing upon the Ways of Coping with Joblessness." *American Journal of Economics and Sociology* 40 (2): 151-63.

Wienk, R.E., C.E. Reid, J.C. Simonson, and F.J. Eggers. 1979. *Measuring Discrimination in American Housing Markets: The Housing Market Practices Survey.* Washington, D.C.: U.S. Department of Housing and Urban Development.

Williams, J., and J. Allen. 1990. "Candid Talk about Quotas: Are Both Sides Being Dishonest about What They're After?" *Washington Post*, December 8, pp. K1, K4.

Yinger, J. 1991a. *Housing Discrimination Study: Incidence and Severity of Unfavorable Treatment*. Washington, D.C.: Urban Institute.

Yinger, J. 1991b. *Housing Discrimination Study: Incidence of Discrimination and Variation in Discriminatory Behavior*. Washington, D.C.: Urban Institute.

DATE DUE
